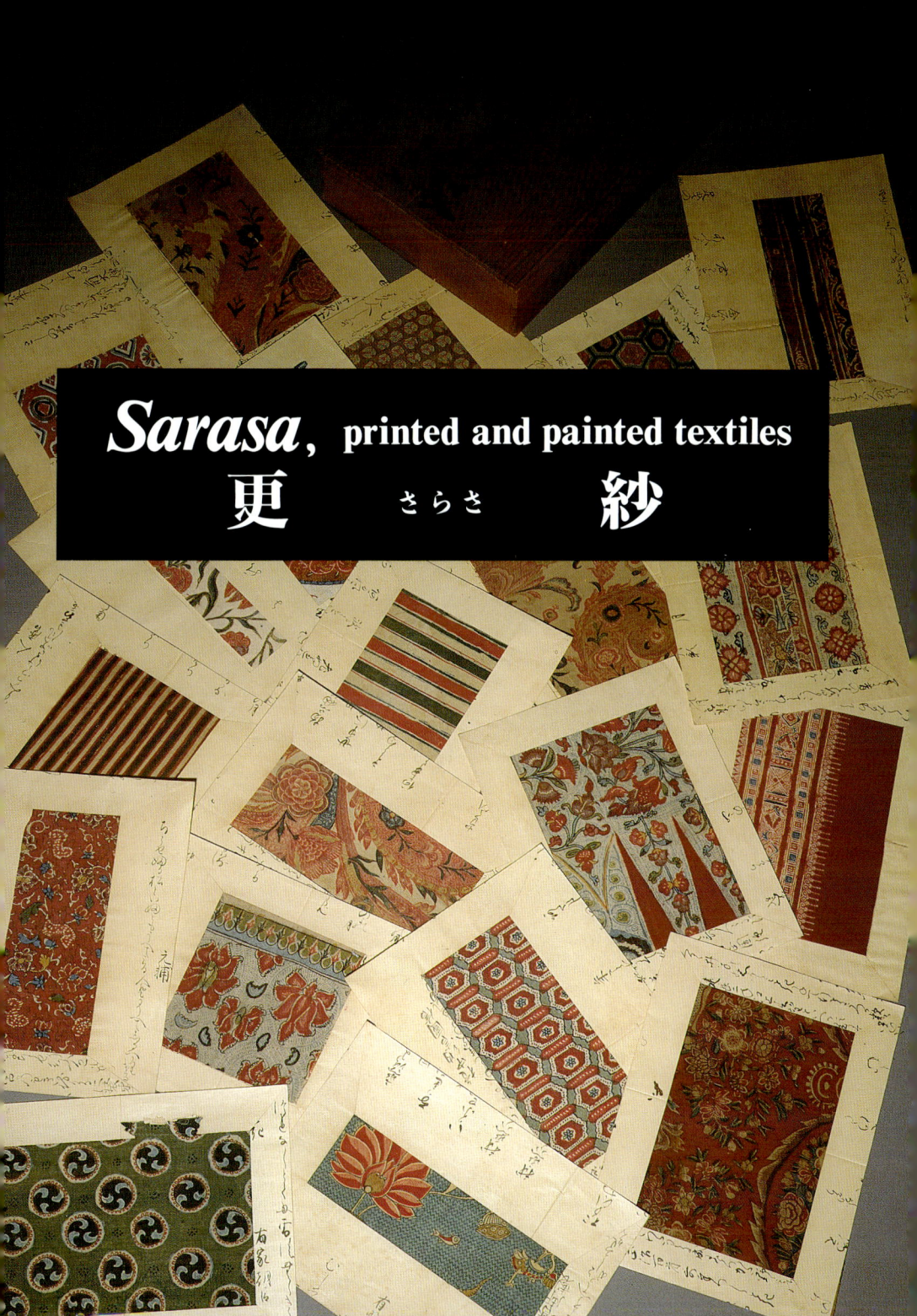

Sarasa, printed and painted textiles
更 さらさ 紗

目次 Contents

インド産インド国内使用　Indian *Sarasa*-chintz ———— 3

インド産フォスタート出土
　　　Made in India Found at Fostat, Egypt ———— 16

インド産ヨーロッパ渡り
　　　Made in India for the European Market ———— 18

インド産シャム渡り
　　　Made in India for the Thai Market ———— 20

インド産インドネシア渡り
　　　Made in India for the Indonesian Market ———— 24

インド産日本古渡り
　　　Made in India for the Japanese Market ———— 32

ヨーロッパ産　Made in Europe ———— 72

和更紗　Made in Japan ———— 78

ペルシャ産　Made in Persia ———— 82

インドネシア産　Made in Indonesia; *Batik* ———— 84

インド更紗の染色法
　　　Dyeing Technique for Indian *Sarasa*-chintz ———— 86

更紗について　吉岡幸雄 ———— 88

***Sarasa*, printed and painted textiles**
　　　　　YOSHIOKA Sachio ———— 92

インド産 インド国内使用

インドで発明された更紗の染色技法は二千年もの歴史を誇っているが、インド国内に現存するのは16世紀以後のものである。回教の色濃いムガール王朝のもので意匠にもそれを反映したもの、あるいはクリシュナ物語のような古典文学に題材をとった図様が多く見られる。こうした更紗はマハラジャの宮殿や旅行用テントの内装、あるいは寺院の掛物として装飾的に使われた。

Indian *sarasa*-chintz

The history of Indian *sarasa*-chintz extends back 2000 years. The pieces in existence today in India were made in and after the 16th century. Most of the designs were inspired by the Islamic culture of the Mughal Empire and by classical literature which includes the tale of Krishna. The fabrics were used to decorate the maharajah's palace, the inside of tents used during travel, and as tapestries adorning Indian temples.

1 藍地草花人物動物文様金雲母更紗
Wall hanging with design of flowers, figures and animals on an indigo blue ground. Cotton: printed, painted, mordant-dyed, wax-resist, and gold and mica-gilded.
17-18c.　193.3×137.0cm

2 白地草花人物鳥獣文様更紗
大阪・鐘紡繊維美術館
Wall hanging with design of flowers, figures, birds and animals on a white ground.
Cotton: printed, painted, mordant-dyed and wax-resist.
17-18c.　225.0×242.0cm
Kanebō Museum of Textiles, Osaka.

4 赤地華桎人物文様金雲母更紗
Wall hanging with design of figures framed by a floral lattice on an indigo blue ground. Cotton: printed, painted, mordant-dyed, wax-resist, gold and mica-gilded.
17-18c.

3 藍地草花人物鳥獣文様金更紗
Wall hanging with design of flowers, figures, birds and animals on an indigo blue ground. Cotton: printed, painted, mordant-dyed, wax-resist and gold-gilded.
17-18c.　126.5×79.0cm

5 白地唐花文様金雲母更紗敷物
Carpet with design of Chinese-style flowers on a white ground.
Cotton: printed, painted, mordant-dyed, wax-resist, gold and mica-gilded. 17-18c. 48.0×66.5cm

6　緑地天使文樣更紗
Wall hanging with design of angels on a green ground.
Cotton: printed, painted, mordant-dyed, and wax-resist.　17-18c.　226.2×216.4cm

7 白地水仙文様更紗
Fragment with design of narcissus on a white ground.
Cotton: printed, painted, mordant-dyed and wax-resist. 17-18c.

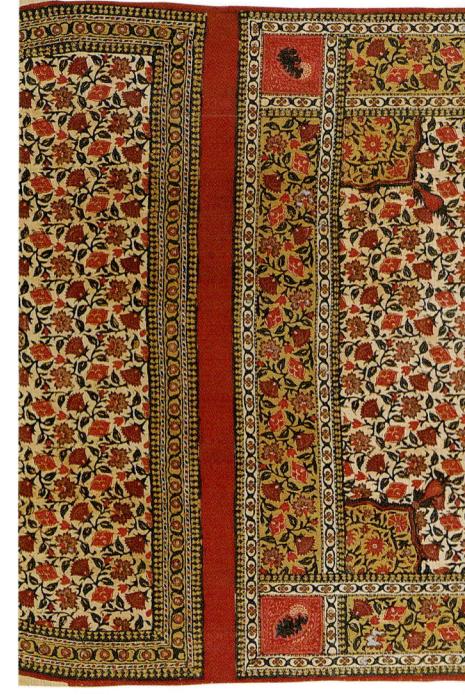

8 　白地草花文様更紗
Cloth with design of flowers on a white ground.
Cotton: printed, painted, mordant-dyed and wax-resisted.　17-18c.　Length:343.5cm

9 茜地華樹文様更紗
Wall hanging with design of flowers on a madder red ground. Cotton: painted, mordant-dyed and wax-resist. 17-18c. 226.0×99.0cm

10 茜地華樹文様更紗
Wall hanging with design of blossoming tree on a madder red ground.
Cotton: painted, mordant-dyed and wax-resist. 17-18c.
364.0×150.0cm

インド産
フォスタート出土

回教圏となったエジプトにおいて、通商都市として繁栄したカイロの郊外フォスタートからは数多くのインド更紗が発掘される。年代的には13、14世紀から18世紀頃にわたるものがあり、技法や意匠も多様である。早くからインド更紗が貿易品として輸出されていたと考えられる。

Made in India Found at Fostat, Egypt

Many pieces of Indian *sarasa*-chintz were found at Fostat, a commercial city strongly influenced by Islam which prospered in ancient Egypt. Dating back from the 13th to 18th centuries, the pieces vary in design and dyeing technique, an indication that Indian *sarasa*-chintz was exported from quite early times.

12 藍地格子花文様更紗
Fragment with design of checker pattern and flowers on an indigo blue ground.
Cotton: painted, mordant-dyed, printed, and wax-resist.   15c.?

13 茜地幾何学文様更紗　兵庫・神戸市立博物館
Fragment with design of geometrical pattern on a madder red ground.
Cotton: printed, painted and mordant-dyed. 15c.?
Kōbe City Museum, Hyōgo

11 茜地水玉文様更紗
Fragment with design of dots on a madder red ground.
Cotton: printed, painted and mordant-dyed. 15c.?

インド産ヨーロッパ渡り

大航海時代にインドへ上陸したヨーロッパ人たちは、初めて見る木綿布の便利さを知ることとなったが、それに赤で彩色された華やかな草花文の更紗には一層魅力を感じ、本国へ持ち帰ったところ爆発的な人気を博した。インド東部のコロマンデル海岸ではヨーロッパ人好みの文様を注文で作り、その輸出に貢献したのである。

Made in India for the European Market

Europeans who landed in India during the "great age of navigation," were attracted to this useful textile from the first glance. The popularity of the red floral-patterned *sarasa*-chintz literally "exploded" when it reached Europe. *Sarasa*-chintz for the European market was produced on the Coromandel Coast, the east coast of India.

15　白地草花人物鳥獣文様更紗
Bedcover with design of flowers, figures, birds and animals on a white ground.
Cotton: painted, mordant-dyed and wax-resist.
17-18c.　353.0×352.5cm

14　白地草花鳥獣文様更紗
Wall hanging with design of flowers, birds and animals on a white ground.
Cotton: painted, mordant-dyed wax-resist.
17-18c.　270.0×154.5cm

インド産 シャム渡り

シャム更紗と通称されているものは、文様がタイの仏教寺院にふさわしく意匠化され、高度な技法で繊細な線が表わされた高級なものである。これもインド、コロマンデル海岸でタイ向きに作られたのであるが、日本の17世紀の文献には「暹羅染(シャムロゾメ)」という記載もあり、わが国へも古くよりもたらされたことが知られる。

Made in India for the Thai Market

A category of Indian *sarasa*-chintz generally called "Siam sarasa" refers to high quality fabrics characterized by elaborate lines and Buddhist designs. It was produced on the Coromandel Coast primarily for the Thai market. However, an old record from 17th century Japan contains a description of "Shamurozome," indicating that Siam *sarasa* also reached Japan from early times.

16 黒地仏に草花獅子文様更紗
兵庫・神戸市立博物館
Wall hanging with design of Buddha, flowers and lions on a black ground.
Cotton: painted, mordant-dyed and wax-resist.
17-18c.　413.0×140.0cm
Kōbe City Museum, Hyōgo.

17 緑地仏に動物文様更紗
Wall hanging with design of Buddha and mythical animals on a green ground.
Cotton: painted, mordant-dyed, and wax-resist.　17-18c.　162.0×94.0cm

18 藍地仏幾何学文様更紗
Wall hanging with design of Buddha and geometrical pattern on an indigo blue green ground.
Cotton: painted, mordant-dyed and wax-resist. 17-18c.

インド産 インドネシア渡り

インドネシア方面にもインド更紗の輸出は盛んだったようで、現在もそれらの更紗が各地から発見される。トラジャ地方のものはやや稚拙で粗い木綿布、バリ島からは戦争の図、スマトラ島ランプンからは日本への古渡り更紗と同様のものと、地域によって品質や文様などに違いがあることは興味深い。

Made in India for the Indonesian Market

Sarasa-chintz imported from Indian is also found in Indonesia. Quality and design differ depending on localities. Those found in the Tradja region lack refinment; those found in Bali have many war motifs; and those found in Lampung (Sumatra), resemble those that reached Japan.

19 茜地パトラ写し文様更紗
Fragment with geometrical design done in double ikat (*patola*) on a madder red ground. Cotton: printed, painted, and mordant-dyed. 17-18c.

20 藍地草花文様更紗（トラジャ族使用）
Wall hanging with design of flowers on an indigo blue ground. (Used by the Toradja tribe)
Cotton: painted, printed, mordant-dyed and wax-resist.
17c.　75.8×252.2cm

21 白地人物戦争文様更紗
Wall hanging with design of a battle on a white ground.
Cotton: painted, printed and mordant-dyed.
17-18c.

23 格子幾何学文様更紗
Fragment with design of checker and geometrical patterns.
Cotton: printed, painted, mordant-dyed and wax-resist. 17-18c.

22 茜地幾何学文様更紗
Fragment with design of geometrical pattern on a madder red ground.
Cotton: painted, mordant-dyed and wax-resist. 17c.

24 藍地草花文樣更紗
Fragment with design of flowers on an indigo blue ground.
Cotton: printed, painted, mordant-dyed and wax-resist. 17-18c.

25 藍・茜地草花文様更紗
Fragment with design of flowers on an indigo blue and madder red ground.
Cotton: printed, painted, mordant-dyed and wax-resist. 17-18c.

インド産
日本古渡り

インド更紗の日本への本格的な輸出は17世紀、オランダの東インド会社によって始められたと考えられている。扇面、小花文、縞などいかにも日本向きの文様と思われるものが多いが、大名家や旧家にはシャム、ランプン、ヨーロッパ向きの文様も伝来している。異国情緒を楽しみながら茶道の仕覆などに使われたのであろう。

Made in India for the Japanese Market

The full-fledged export of Indian *sarasa*-chintz to Japan seems to have been undertaken by the Dutch United East Indian Company (V.O.C.) in the 17th century. The designs, such as stripes, small floral patterns, and fans reflect Japanese taste. Interestingly, designs for Siam, Lampung and Europe are also found adorning *shifuku* (cloth cases for the containers of powdered green tea) which have been preserved in *daimyō* and old families of high social ranking who appreciated the exotic qualities of this fabric.

27 薄藍地花幾何学鋸歯文様更紗
Fragment with design of flowers, geometrical and sawtooth pattern on a light indigo blue ground. Cotton: painted, mordant-dyed and wax-resist). 17c.

26 白地草花鋸歯文様更紗
Fukusa (square wrapper) with design of flowers and sawtooth pattern on a white ground.
Cotton: painted, mordant-dyed and wax-resist. 17c.　36.0×31.9cm

28 白地縞花鳥鋸歯文様更紗
Fragment with design of stripes, flowers, birds and sawtooth pattern on a white ground. Cotton: painted, mordant-dyed and wax-resist. 17c.

29 白地草花文様更紗 （尾張徳川家伝来）
愛知・徳川美術館
Fragment with design of flowers on a white ground.
Cotton: painted, mordant-dyed and wax-resist.
17c.
Provenance: Tokugawa family
Tokugawa Art Museum, Aichi.

30 黄地草花文様更紗 （尾張徳川家伝来）
愛知・徳川美術館
Fragment with design of flowers on a yellow ground.
Cotton: painted, mordant-dyed and wax-resist.
17-18c.
Provenance: Tokugawa family
Tokugawa Art Museum, Aichi.

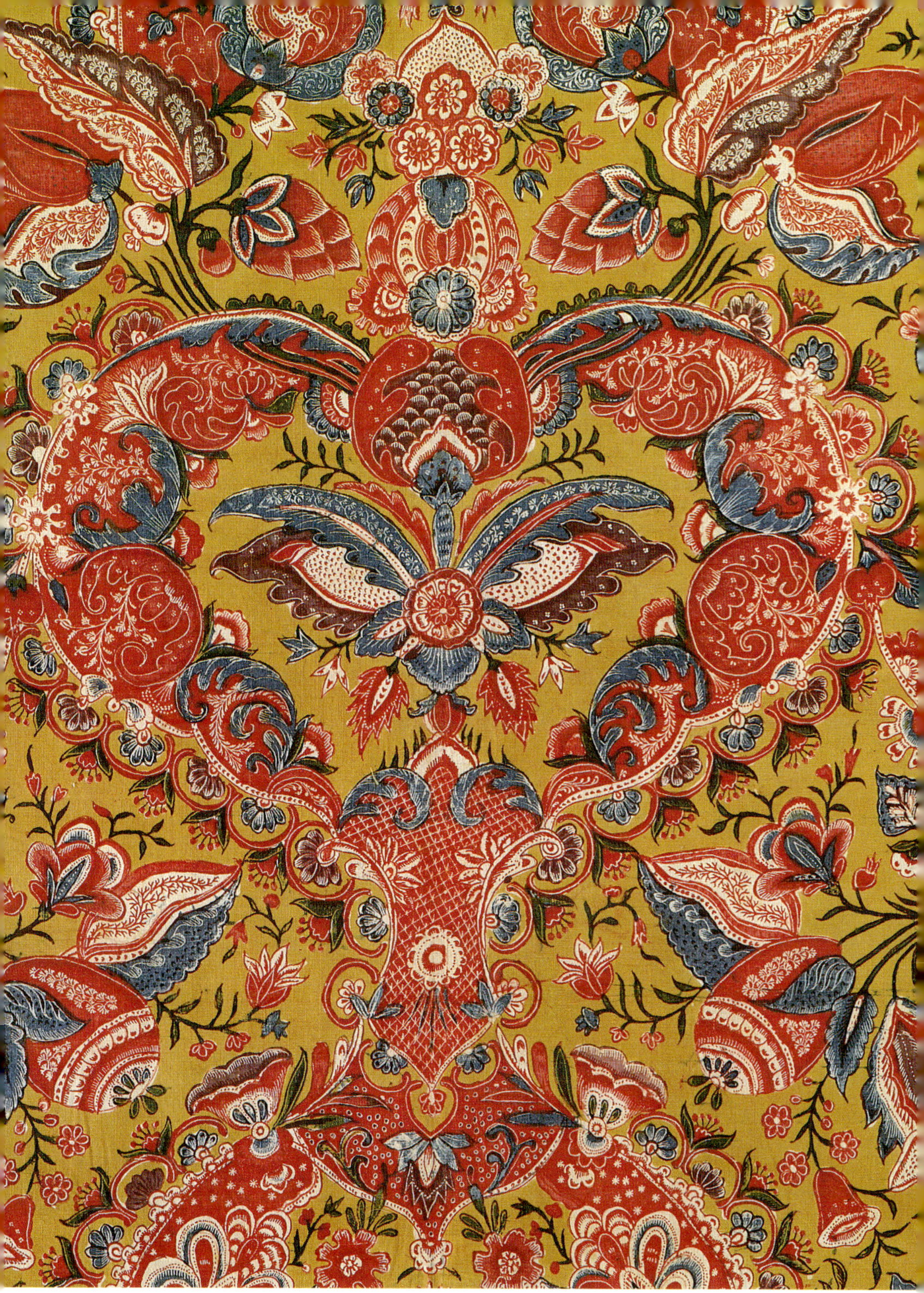

31

32   33   34

36

35

35 緑地草花文様更紗
Fragment with design of flowers on a green ground. Cotton: painted, mordant-dyed and wax-resist.　17-18c.

36 白地草花虫文様更紗
Fragment with design of flowers and insects on a white ground. Cotton: painted, mordant-dyed and wax-resist.　17-18c.

31 藍地草花文様更紗
Fragment with design of flowers on an indigo blue ground. Cotton: painted, mordant-dyed and wax-resist.　17-18c.

32 白地草花鳥蝶文様更紗（赤星家伝来）
Fragment with design of flowers, birds and butterflies on a white ground. Cotton: painted, mordant-dyed and wax-resist.　17-18c. Provenance: Akaboshi family

33 白地草花文様金更紗（赤星家伝来）
Fragment with design of flowers on a white ground. Cotton: painted, mordant-dyed and gold-gilded.　17-18c. Provenance: Akaboshi family

34 白地草花文様更紗（赤星家伝来）
Fragment with design of flowers on a white ground. Cotton: painted, mordant-dyed and wax-resist.　17-18c. Provenance: Akaboshi family

36

彦根更紗

近江の彦根藩井伊家に伝来した一群の更紗裂は「彦根更紗」と呼ばれる。その大半は古渡りのインド更紗で、江戸時代の見本帖などに描かれた文様のほとんどを見出すことができる。

Hikone *Sarasa*

"Hikone Sarasa" refers to a collection of *sarasa*-chintz which has been handed down in the Ii family, the *daimyō* of Hikone province in feudal Japan. Most of the fabrics were brought to Japan in the 17th and 18th centuries. They cover almost all the *sarasa* designs contained in sample books.

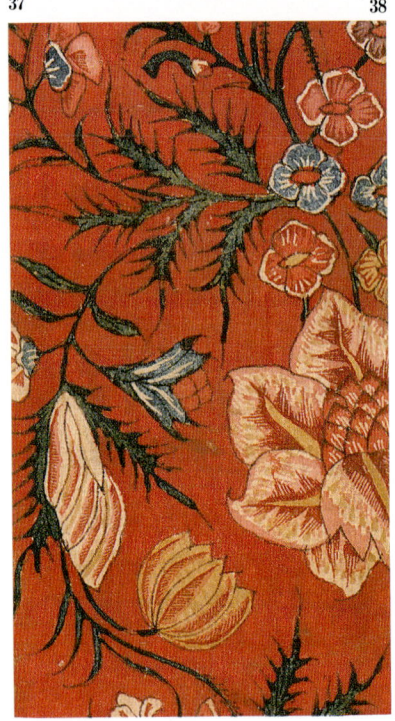

37 38 39

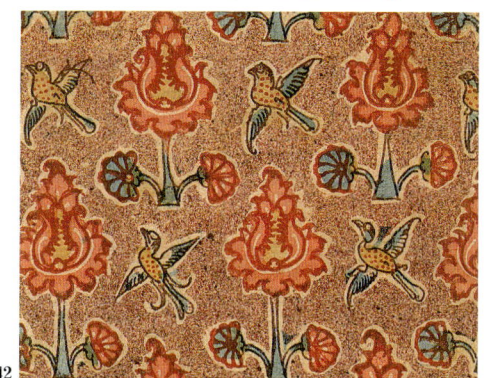

37 **白地縞花文様更紗**（井伊家伝来）
東京国立博物館
Fragment with design of stripes and flowers on a white ground. Cotton: painted, mordant-dyed and wax-resist.　17-18c. Provenance: Ii family
Tokyo National Museum

38 **赤地花文様更紗**（井伊家伝来）
東京国立博物館
Fragment with design of flowers on a red ground. Cotton: painted, mordant-dyed and wax-resist.　17-18c. Provenance: Ii family
Tokyo National Museum.

39 **白地花唐草文様更紗**（井伊家伝来）
東京国立博物館
Fragment with design of flowers and arabesque on a white ground. Cotton: painted, mordant-dyed and wax-resist.　17-18c. Provenance: Ii family
Tokyo National Museum.

40 **白地雲鳥文様更紗**（井伊家伝来）
東京国立博物館
Fragment with design of clouds and birds on a white ground. Cotton: painted, mordant-dyed and wax-resist.　17-18c. Provenance: Ii family
Tokyo National Museum.

41 **浅葱地蓮水禽文様更紗**（井伊家伝来）
東京国立博物館
Fragment with design of lotus and waterfowl on a pale green ground. Cotton: painted, mordant-dyed and wax-resist.　17-18c. Provenance: Ii family
Tokyo National Museum.

42 **紫霜降地花鳥文様更紗**（井伊家伝来）
東京国立博物館
Fragment with design of flowers and birds on a mottled purple ground. Cotton: painted, mordant-dyed and wax-resist.　17-18c. Provenance: Ii family
Tokyo National Museum.

43 **赤紫地松鳥文様更紗**（井伊家伝来）
東京国立博物館
Fragment with design of pine trees and birds on a purple red ground. Cotton: painted, mordant-dyed and wax-resist.　17-18c. Provenance: Ii family
Tokyo National Museum.

祇園祭装飾の更紗

五百年以上もの歴史を誇る京都の祇園祭。江戸時代に至ってそれを担う町衆が富を蓄えるようになり、山、鉾の装飾に華麗な輸入絨緞、更紗などが使われた。なかでも南観音山に伝来する中国風の山水文様は、同種のものがかつてオランダ（現在はアメリカ、クーパー・ヒューウィット博物館）にもあったことがわかり、注目されている一点である。

Sarasa Hanging for the Gion Festival

The citizens of Kyoto who sponsored the Gion Festival became so rich in the Edo period that they were able to decorate their floats with luxurious carpets of foreign origin and *sarasa* hangings. The hanging for the Minami-kannonyama Float is important in that it closely resembles one preserved in the collections of the Cooper Hewitt Museum in New York.

44　茜地鶴松山水文様更紗（祇園祭南観音山前掛）
京都・南観音山保存会
Hanging of Minami-kannonyama Float for Gion Festival with design of cranes, pine-trees and landscape on a madder red ground.
Cotton: painted, mordant-dyed and wax-resisted. 17-18c. Made in Edo period.
206.0×250.0cm
Minami-kannonyama Festival Preservation Society, Kyoto.

45

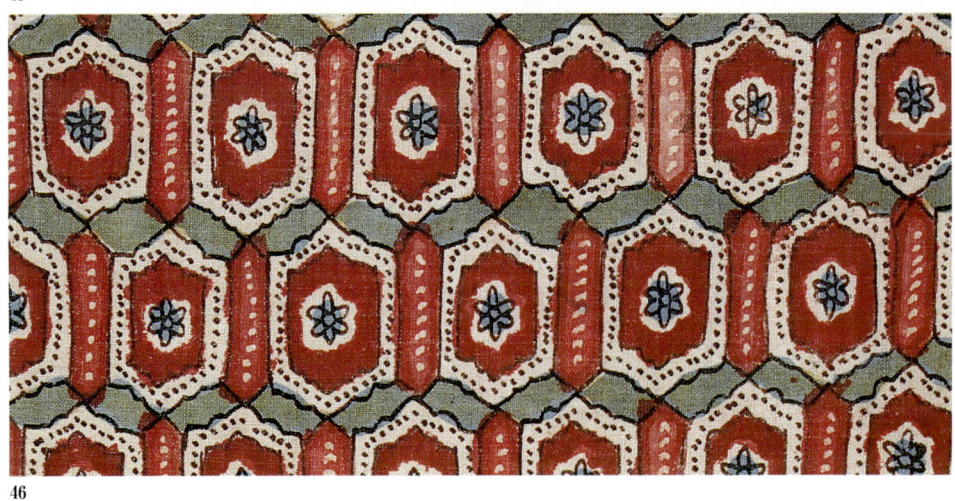

46

45 白地花入り亀甲文様更紗
Fragment with design of tortoise shell pattern.
Cotton: painted, mordant-dyed and wax-resist.
17-18c.

46 白地花入り亀甲文様更紗（赤星家伝来）
Fragment with design of tortoise shell pattern.
Cotton: painted, mordant-dyed and wax-resist.
17-18c.
Provenance : Akaboshi family

47 緑地五徳文様更紗 （赤星家伝来）
Fragment with design of triple commas on a green ground.
Cotton: painted, mordant-dyed and wax-resist.
17-18c.
Provenance : Akaboshi family

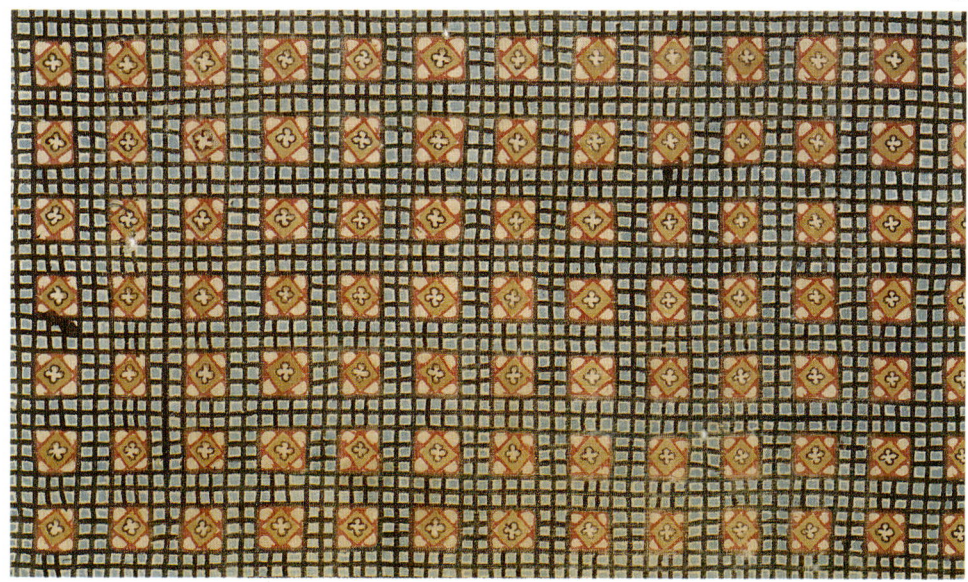

48 白地格子文様更紗
Fragment with design of checker pattern on a white ground.
Cotton: painted, mordant-dyed and wax-resist.
17-18c.

49

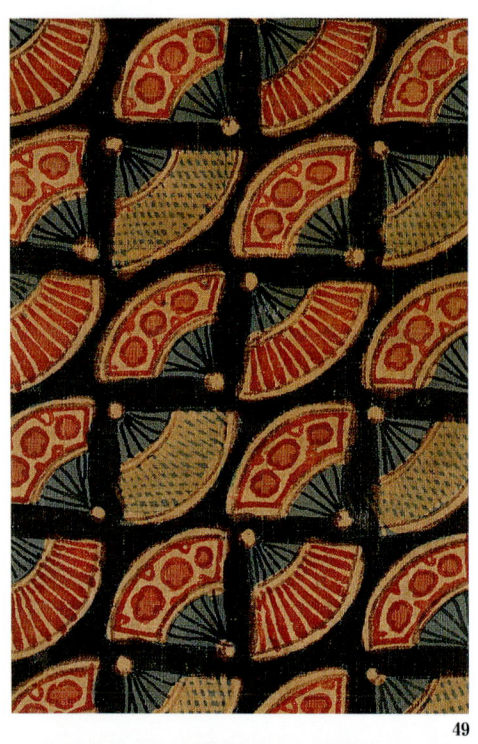

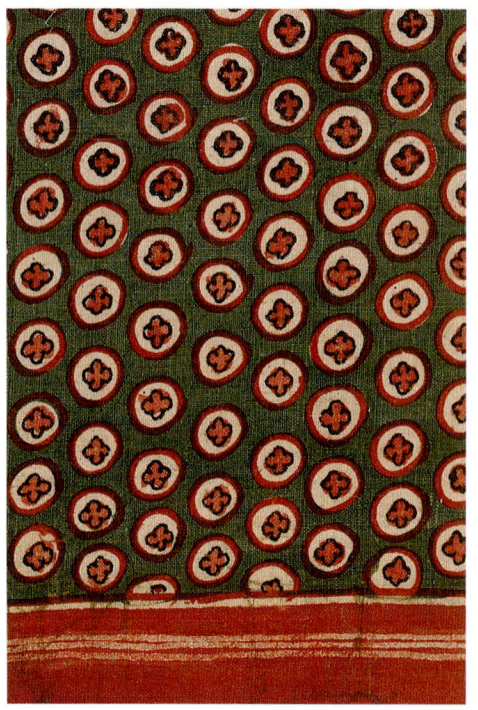

50

51

52

49 藍地扇文様更紗（井伊家伝来）
東京国立博物館
Fragment with design of fans on an indigo blue ground. Cotton: painted, mordant-dyed and wax-resist. 17-18c. Provenance: Ii family
Tokyo National Museum.

50 花入格子文様更紗（井伊家伝来）
東京国立博物館
Fragment with design of flowers in the checker pattern. Cotton: painted, mordant-dyed and wax-resist. 17-18c.
Provenance: Ii family
Tokyo National Museum.

51 黒地丸紋文様更紗（井伊家伝来）
東京国立博物館
Fragment with design of roundels on a black ground. Cotton: painted, mordant-dyed and wax-resist. 17-18c. Provenance: Ii family
Tokyo National Museum.

52 萌葱地丸紋文様更紗（井伊家伝来）
東京国立博物館
Fragment with design of roundels on light green ground. Cotton: painted, mordant-dyed and wax-resist. 17-18c. Provenance: Ii family
Tokyo National Museum.

53 花菱格子文様更紗（井伊家伝来）
東京国立博物館
Fragment with design of flowers lozenge pattern. Cotton: painted, mordant-dyed and wax-resist. 17-18c. Provenance: Ii family
Tokyo National Museum.

54 藍地格子丸文様更紗（井伊家伝来）
東京国立博物館
Fragment with design of checker and circular pattern on an indigo blue ground. Cotton: painted, mordant-dyed and wax-resist. 17-18c.
Provenance: Ii family
Tokyo National Museum.

55 白地菊花網文様更紗（井伊家伝来）
東京国立博物館
Fragment with design of crysanthemums and net pattern on a white ground. Cotton: painted, mordant-dyed and wax-resist. 17-18c.
Provenance: Ii family
Tokyo National Museum.

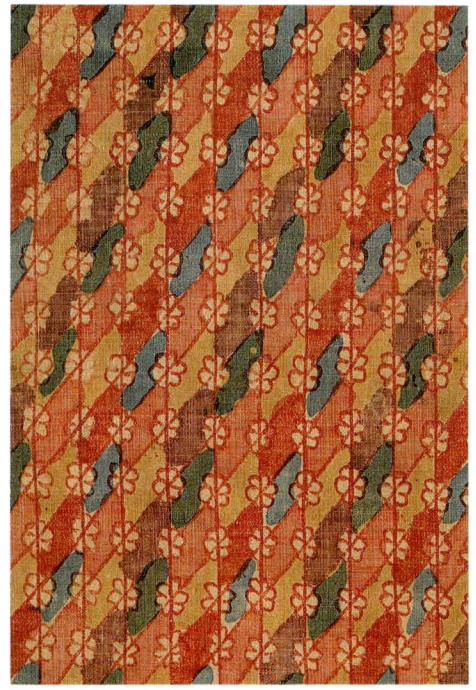

53

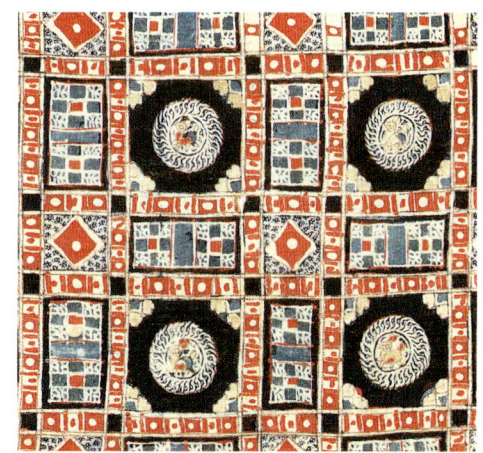

54

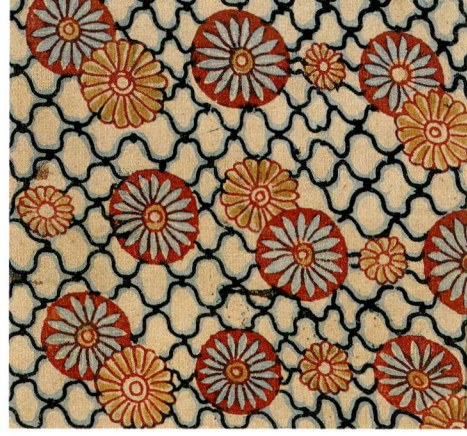

55

56 白地縞文様更紗（赤星家伝来）
Fragment with design of stripes on a white ground. Cotton: painted, mordant-dyed and wax-resist. 17-18c. Provenance: Akaboshi family

57 白地縞文様更紗
Fragment with design of stripes on a white ground. Cotton: painted, mordant-dyed and wax-resist. 17-18c.

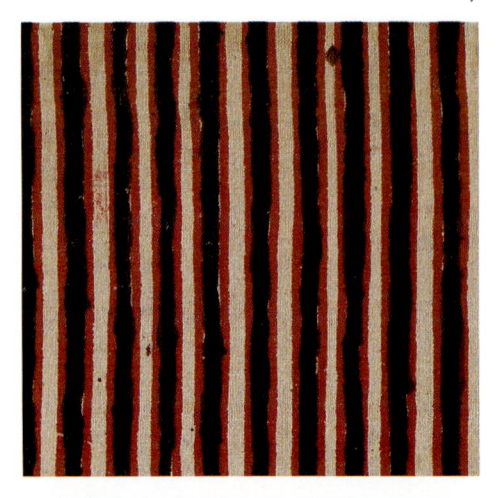

58 白地縞花唐草文様更紗
Fragment with design of stripes, flowers and arabesque on a white ground. Cotton: painted, mordant-dyed and wax-resist. 17-18c.

59 白地縞文様更紗
Fragment with design of stripes on a white ground. Cotton: painted, mordant-dyed and wax-resist. 17-18c.

60 白地縞幾何学文様更紗（井伊家伝来）
東京国立博物館
Fragment with design of stripes and geometrical pattern on a white ground. Cotton: painted, mordant-dyed and wax-resist. 17-18c.
Provenance: Ii family
Tokyo National Museum.

61 白地縞花唐草文様更紗（井伊家伝来）
東京国立博物館
Fragment with design of stripes, flowers and arabesque on a white ground. Cotton: painted, mordant-dyed and wax-resist. 17-18c.
Provenance: Ii family
Tokyo National Museum.

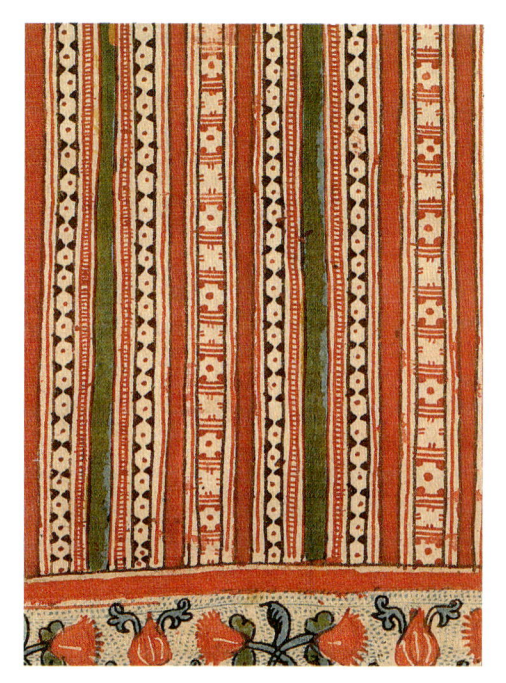

62 白地縞花唐草文様更紗（井伊家伝来）
東京国立博物館
Fragment with design of stripes, flowers and arabesque on a white ground. Cotton: painted, mordant-dyed and wax-resist. 17-18c.
Provenance: Ii family
Tokyo National Museum.

64 茜地幾何学文様更紗（三井家伝来）
Fragment with design of geometrical pattern on a madder red ground. Cotton: painted, mordant-dyed and wax-resist. 17c.
Provenance: Mitsui family

63 藍・茜地絣格子草花文様更紗
Fragment with design of checker pattern and flowers on an indigo blue and a madder red ground with ikat.
Cotton: painted, mordant-dyed and wax-resist. 17-18c.

65 茜地幾何学文様絣入り更紗（井伊家伝来）
東京国立博物館
Fragment with design of geometrical pattern on a madder red ground with ikat.
Cotton: painted, mordant-dyed and wax-resist.
17-18c. Provenance: Ii family
Tokyo National Museum

66 茜地幾何学文様絣入り更紗（井伊家伝来）
東京国立博物館
Fragment with design of geometrical pattern on a madder red ground with ikat.
Cotton: painted, mordant-dyed and wax-resist.
17-18c. Provenance: Ii family
Tokyo National Museum

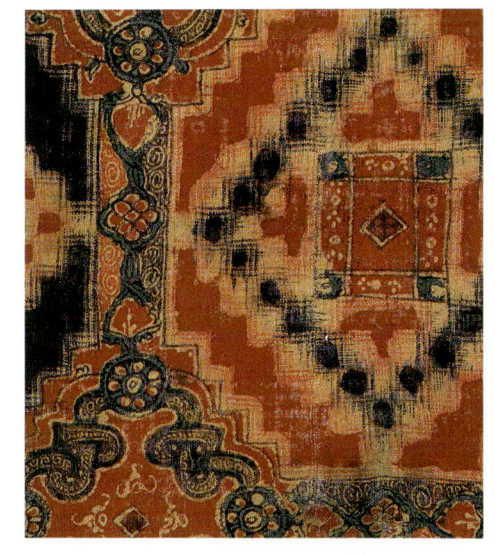

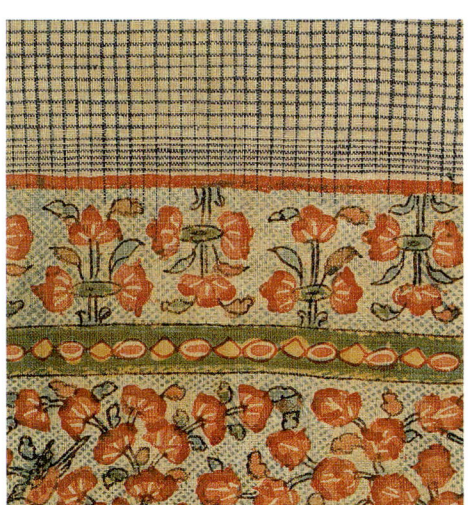

67 白地幾何学文様絣入り更紗（井伊家伝来）
東京国立博物館
Fragment with design of geometrical pattern on a white ground with ikat.
Cotton: painted, mordant-dyed and wax-resist.
17-18c. Provenance: Ii family
Tokyo National Museum

68 茜地幾何学文様絣入り更紗（井伊家伝来）
東京国立博物館
Fragment with design of geometrical pattern on a madder red ground with ikat.
Cotton: painted, mordant-dyed and wax-resist.
17-18c. Provenance: Ii family
Tokyo National Museum

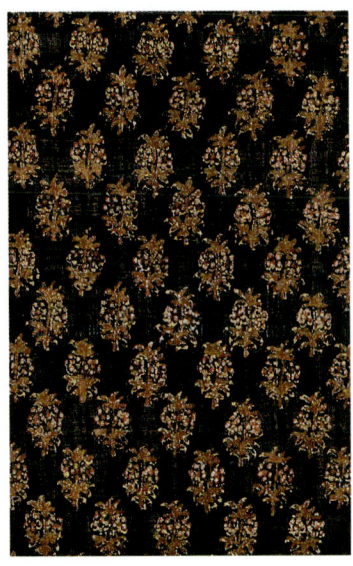

69 黒地草花文様金更紗
Fragment with design of flowers on a black ground.
Cotton: printed, painted, mordant-dyed, wax-resist and gold-gilded. 17-18c.

70 白地草花文様金更紗
Fragment with design of a floral lattice on a white ground.
Cotton: painted, mordant-dyed, wax-resist and gold-gilded. 17-18c.

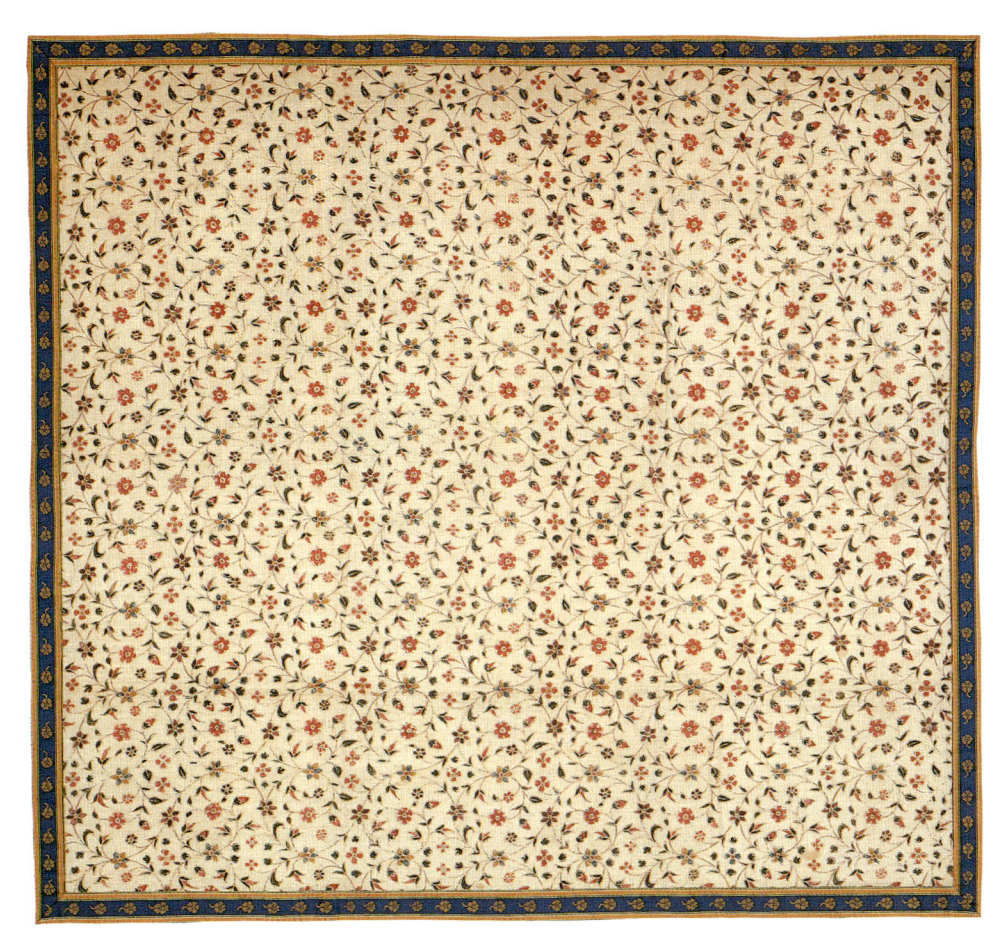

71　白地笹蔓文様金更紗茶具敷
Floor covering for the tea ceremony with design of vine and flowers on a white ground.
Cotton: painted, mordant-dyed, wax-resist and gold-gilded. 17c.　62.0×66.0cm

72　白地草花文様金更紗茶具敷
Floor covering for the tea ceremony with design of flowers on a white ground.
Cotton: painted, mordant-dyed, wax-resist and gold-gilded. 17c.　67.5×82.0cm

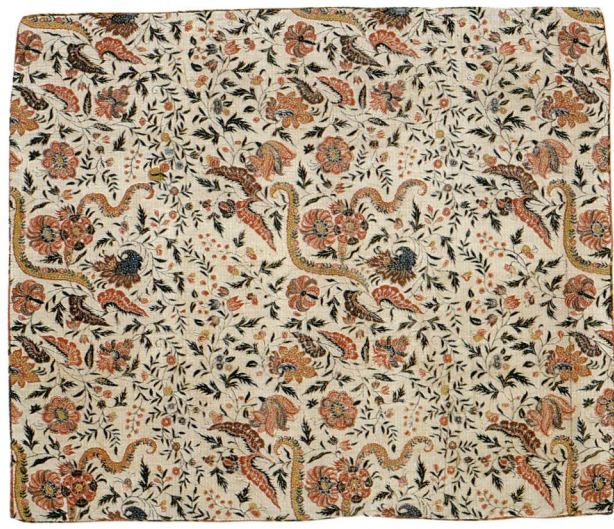

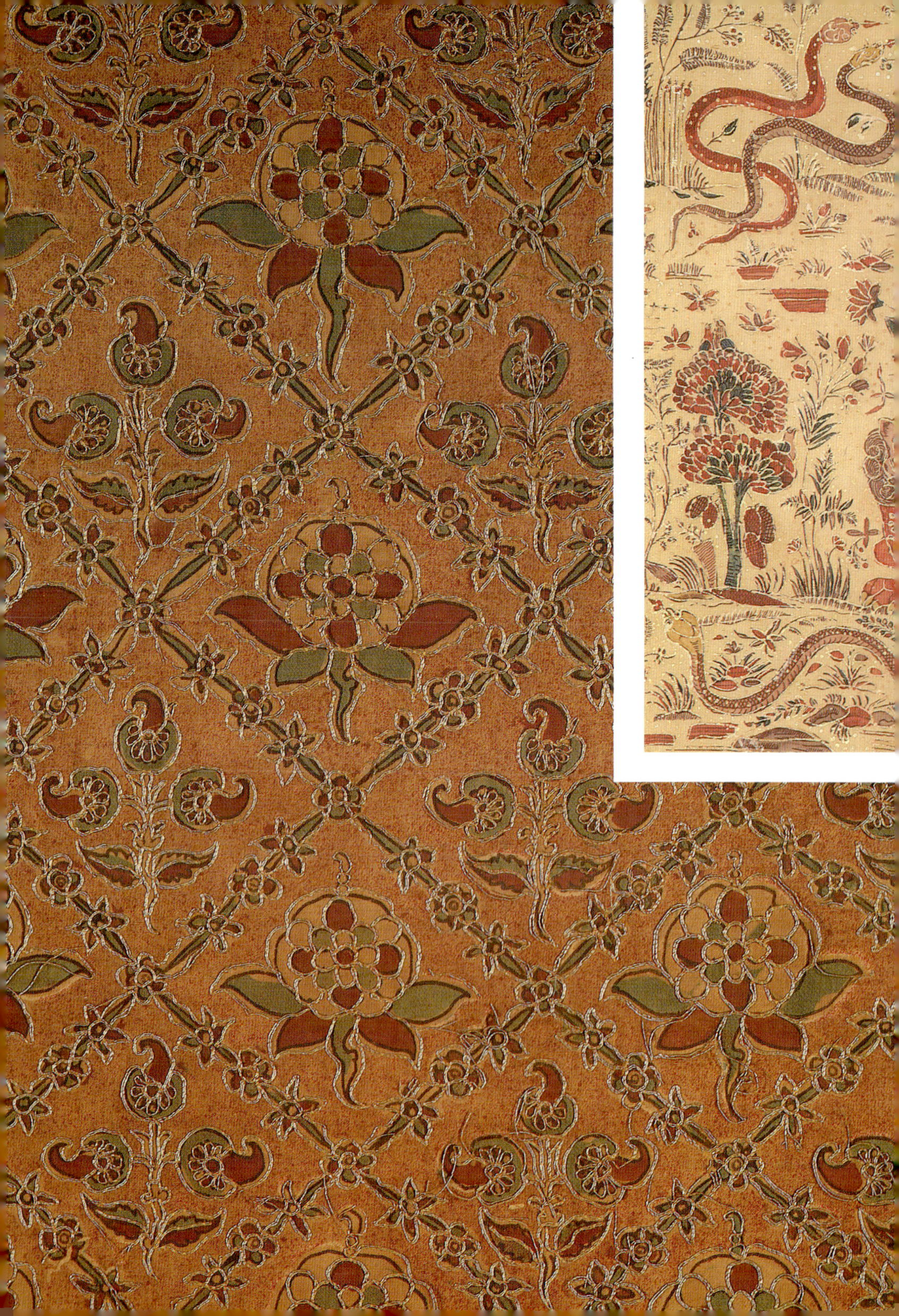

73 白地花格子文様霜降更紗金縫取 （前田家伝来）
京都国立博物館
Fragment with design of flowers on a white ground.
Cotton: painted, mordant-dyed, wax-resist and gold-embroiderd. 17c.
Provenance: Maeda family
Kyoto National Museum

74 白地草花獅子蛇文様金更紗 （前田家伝来）
京都国立博物館
Fragment with design of lions, snakes and flowers on a white ground.
Cotton: painted, mordant-dyed, wax-resist and gold-gilded. 17c.
Provenance: Maeda family
Kyoto National Museum

鬼更紗

粗い木綿布に木版で文様を表わし、茜染された更紗には日本において「鬼更紗」という通称が付けられている。そのほとんどが茜染だけで、臈伏せ藍染の工程が省かれたもので、敷物、祇園祭胴掛などに用いられ親しまれている。

Oni-zarasa

Known in Japan as "oni-zarasa," this *sarasa* is made of coarsely woven cotton and has a woodblock print design that has been rendered in madder red. *Sarasa* of this type was widely used as floor coverings and hangings for the Gion Festival.

75　茜地草花文様鬼更紗敷物（祇園祭南観音山見送り）
　　貞享元年銘　京都・南観音山保存会
Carpet for the Gion Festival Minami-Kannonyama Float with design of flowers on a madder red ground.
Cotton: printed, painted, mordant-dyed and wax-resist. Dated 1684　298.0×177.0cm
Minami-Kannonyama Festival Preservation Society, Kyoto

76　茜地草花文様鬼更紗（祇園祭鯉山胴掛）
　　京都・鯉山保存会
Hanging for the Gion Festival Koiyama Float with design of flowers on a madder red ground.
Cotton: printed, painted, mordant-dyed and wax-resist. 17-18c. Made in Edo period. 108.0×210.0cm
Koiyama Festival Preservation Society, Kyoto

77 茜地草花文様鬼更紗
Fragment with design of flowers on a madder red ground.
Cotton: printed, painted, mordant-dyed, wax-resist and gold-gilded. 17-18c.

78 更紗尽し掛軸（浅見家伝来）
Hanging-scroll, patchwork of Indian chintz.
Cotton: printed, painted, mordant-dyed, wax-resist and mica-gilded.
17c.　112.0×59.0cm
Provenance: Asami family

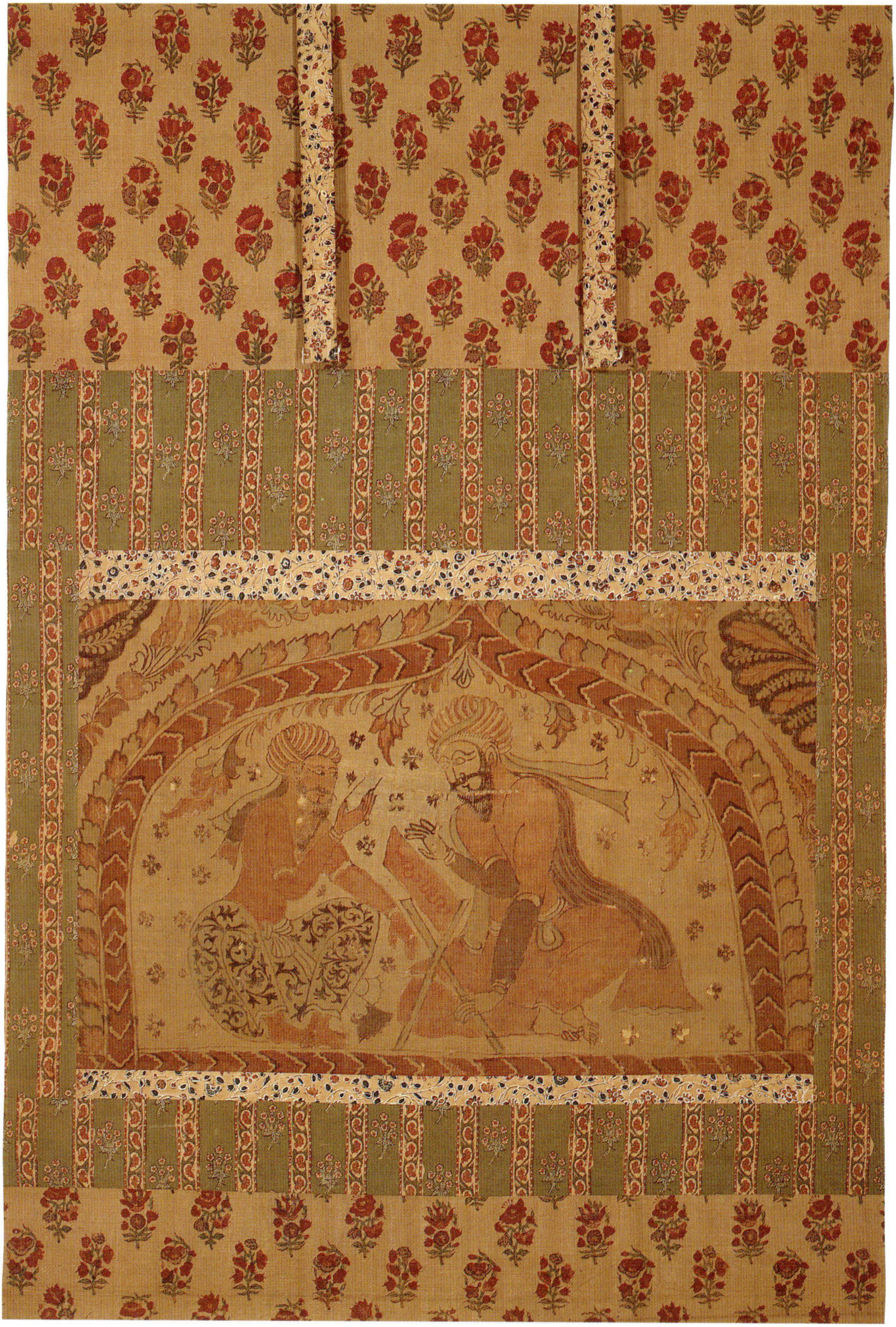

79 更紗杜若文様縫合小袖（三井家伝来） 東京・文化学園服飾博物館
Kosode kimono, patchwork of Indian chintz and Japanese Yūzen with iris design. Silk and cotton: printed, painted, mordant-dyed and wax-resist. 17c. Pieced together in late Edo period.
Provenance: Mitsui family
Bunka Gakuen Costume Museum, Tokyo

80 更紗縫合下着　兵庫・神戸市立博物館
Underwear, patchwork of Indian chintz (17-18c), European prints and Japanese stencil (18-19c.)
Pieced together in Taishō-Meiji period.
Length: 144.0cm
Kōbe City Museum, Hyōgo

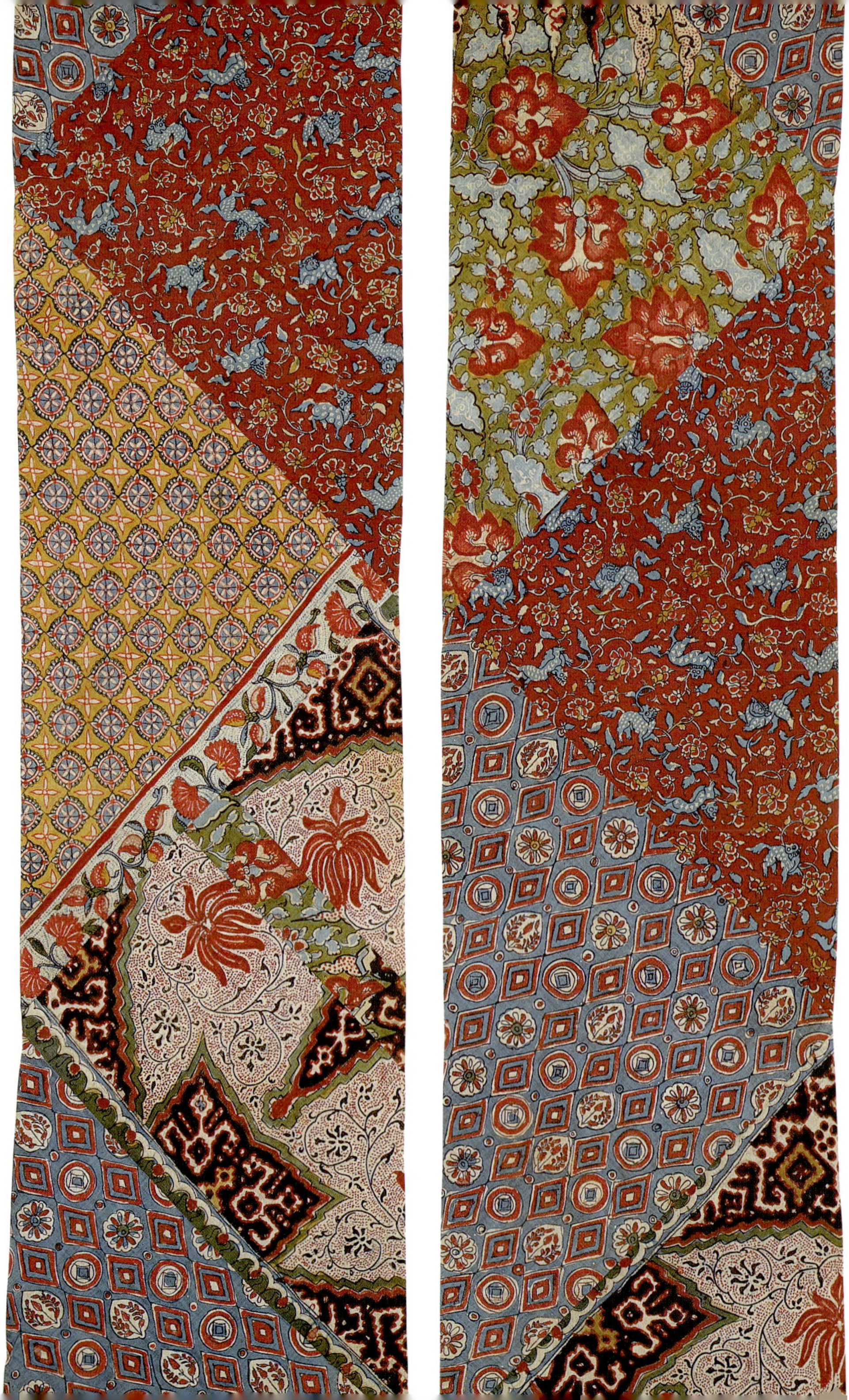

81 更紗縫合帯（三井家伝来）　東京・文化学園服飾博物館
　　Obi (sash), patchwork of Indian chintz. Cotton: painted, mordant-dyed and wax-resist. 17c. Pieced together in late Edo period. Width: 24.5cm Provenance: Mitsui family
　　Bunka Gakuen Costume Museum, Tokyo

82 白地縞草花文様更紗仕覆　茶入　仁清作　大阪・逸翁美術館
　　Cloth case with design of stripes and flowers on a white ground. Cotton: painted, mordant-dyed and wax-resist. 17-18c.　65.0×60.0cm　Tea Container by Ninsei.
　　Itsuō Art Museum, Osaka

83 仕覆　4点
　　Four tea container cloth cases. Cotton: painted, mordant-dyed and wax-resist. 17-18c.

84 85

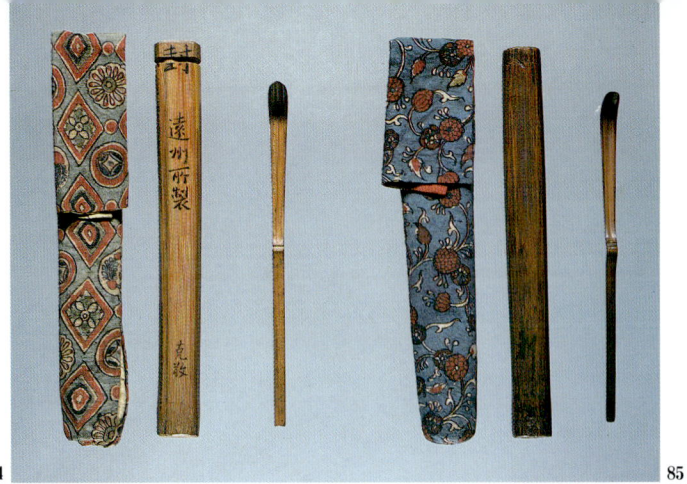

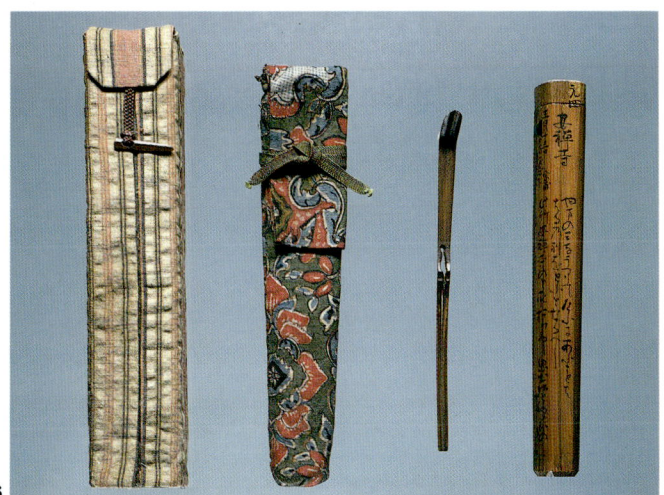

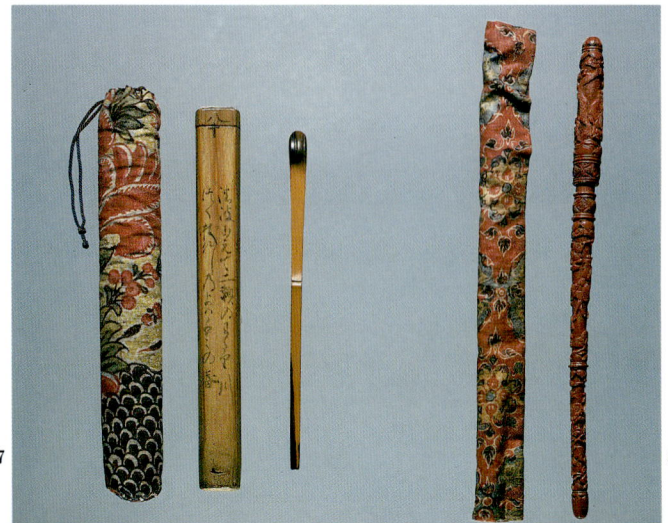

86

87 88

89

84 藍地小花文様更紗袋　茶杓　千利休作　東京・永青文庫
Cloth case with design of flowers on an indigo blue ground. Cotton: painted, mordant-dyed and wax-resist. 17-18c. Made in Edo period. 30.5×4.3cm　Tea Scoop by Sen-no Rikyū. Provenance: Hosokawa family
Eisei Bunko Museum, Tokyo

85 藍地幾何学文様更紗袋　茶杓　小堀遠州作　東京・永青文庫
Cloth case with design of geometrical pattern on an indigo blue ground. Cotton: painted, mordant-dyed and wax-resist. 17-18c. Made in Edo period. 32.5×3.7cm　Tea Scoop by Kobori Enshū. Provenance: Hosokawa family
Eisei Bunko Museum, Tokyo

86 緑地草花文様更紗袋・カピタン裂　茶杓　小堀遠州作　銘安禅寺　東京・永青文庫
Cloth case with design of flowers on a green ground. Cotton: painted, mordant-dyed and wax-resist. 17-18c. Made in Edo period. 32.0×4.2cm　40.0×4.5×4.5cm　Tea Scoop by Kobori Enshū. Provenance: Hosokawa family
Eisei Bunko Museum, Tokyo

87 黄地立木文様更紗袋　茶杓　細川三斎作　歌銘　東京・永青文庫
Cloth case with design of trees on a yellow ground. Cotton: painted, mordant-dyed and wax-resist. 17-18c. Made in Edo period. 21.5×4.0cm　Tea Scoop by Hosokawa Sansai
Eisei Bunko Museum, Tokyo

88 茜地小花文様更紗堆朱山水筆袋　東京・永青文庫
Cloth case for a writing brush with design of flowers on a madder red ground. Cotton: painted, mordant-dyed and wax-resist. 17-18c. Made in Edo period. 27.0×3.0cm Provenance: Hosokawa family
Eisei Bunko Museum, Tokyo

89 白地小花文様更紗袋・カピタン裂　茶杓　佐久間宗可作　銘大むしくひ　東京・永青文庫
Case with design of flowers on a white ground. Cotton: painted, mordant-dyed and wax-resist. 17-18c. Sewing in Edo period.　32.0×4.0cm　22.3×5.0×4.5cm　Tea Scoop by Sakuma Sōka.
Eisei Bunko Museum, Tokyo

90 茜地草花文様更紗腰差したばこ入れ
Tabacco pouch with design of flowers on a madder red ground.
Cotton: painted, mordant-dyed and wax-resist. 17-18c.

91 茜地草花唐草文様更紗たばこ入れ
Tobacco pouch with design of flowers and arabesque on a madder red ground.
Cotton: painted, mordant-dyed and wax-resist. 17-18c.

92 白地草花文様更紗女持ち懐中たばこ入れ
A pair of tobacco pouches for women with design of flowers on a white ground.
Cotton: painted, mordant-dyed and wax-resist. 17-18c.

93 白地動物文様更紗腰差したばこ入れ　東京・たばこと塩の博物館
Tobacco pouch with design of animals on a white ground.
Cotton: painted, mordant-dyed and wax-resist. 17-18c.
Tobacco & Salt Museum, Tokyo

94 臙脂地菱丸文様更紗腰差したばこ入れ　東京・たばこと塩の博物館
Tobacco pouch with design of lozenge and roundel pattern on a cochineal red ground.
Cotton: painted, mordant-dyed and wax-resist. 17-18c.
Tobacco & Salt Museum, Tokyo

95 白地縞文様更紗腰差したばこ入れ　東京・たばこと塩の博物館
Tobacco pouch with design of stripes on a white ground.
Cotton: painted, mordant-dyed and wax-resist. 17-18c.
Tobacco & Salt Museum, Tokyo

96 白地鶏頭文様更紗腰差したばこ入れ　東京・たばこと塩の博物館
Tobacco pouch with design of cockscombs on a white ground.
Cotton: painted, mordant-dyed and wax-resist. 17-18c.
Tobacco & Salt Museum, Tokyo

97 藍地縞鶏頭文様更紗腰差したばこ入れ　東京・たばこと塩の博物館
Tobacco pouch with design of cockscombs and stripes on an indigo blue ground.
Cotton: painted, mordant-dyed and wax-resist. 17-18c.
Tobacco & Salt Museum, Tokyo

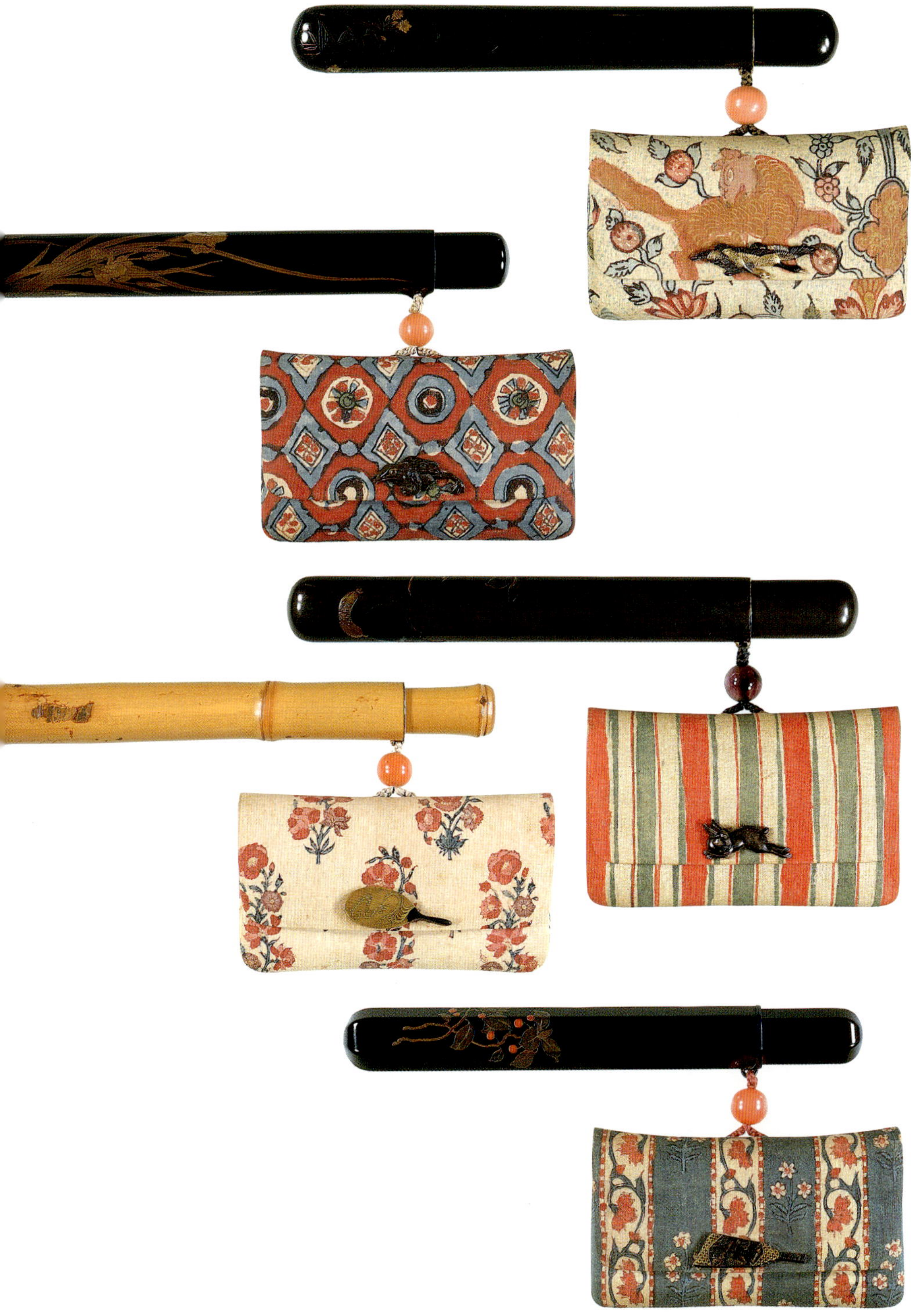

画中の更紗

更紗を衣裳に仕立て着用した例はいくつか散見されるが、それが屏風絵にも描かれている。それも江戸時代前期のものが多く、早くから更紗が愛用されているがことが知られる。

Sarasa in Genre Paintings

Figures wearing *sarasa* kimono appear on folding screens of the early Edo period. This indicates that wearing *sarasa* kimono was popular in those days.

98 誰袖図屏風　六曲一隻　静岡・MOA美術館
Tagasode Screen (Hanging *kosode* Kimono)
Six-fold screen. Color on gold-leafed paper.
Early Edo period. 146.2×363.0cm
MOA Museum of Art, Shizuoka

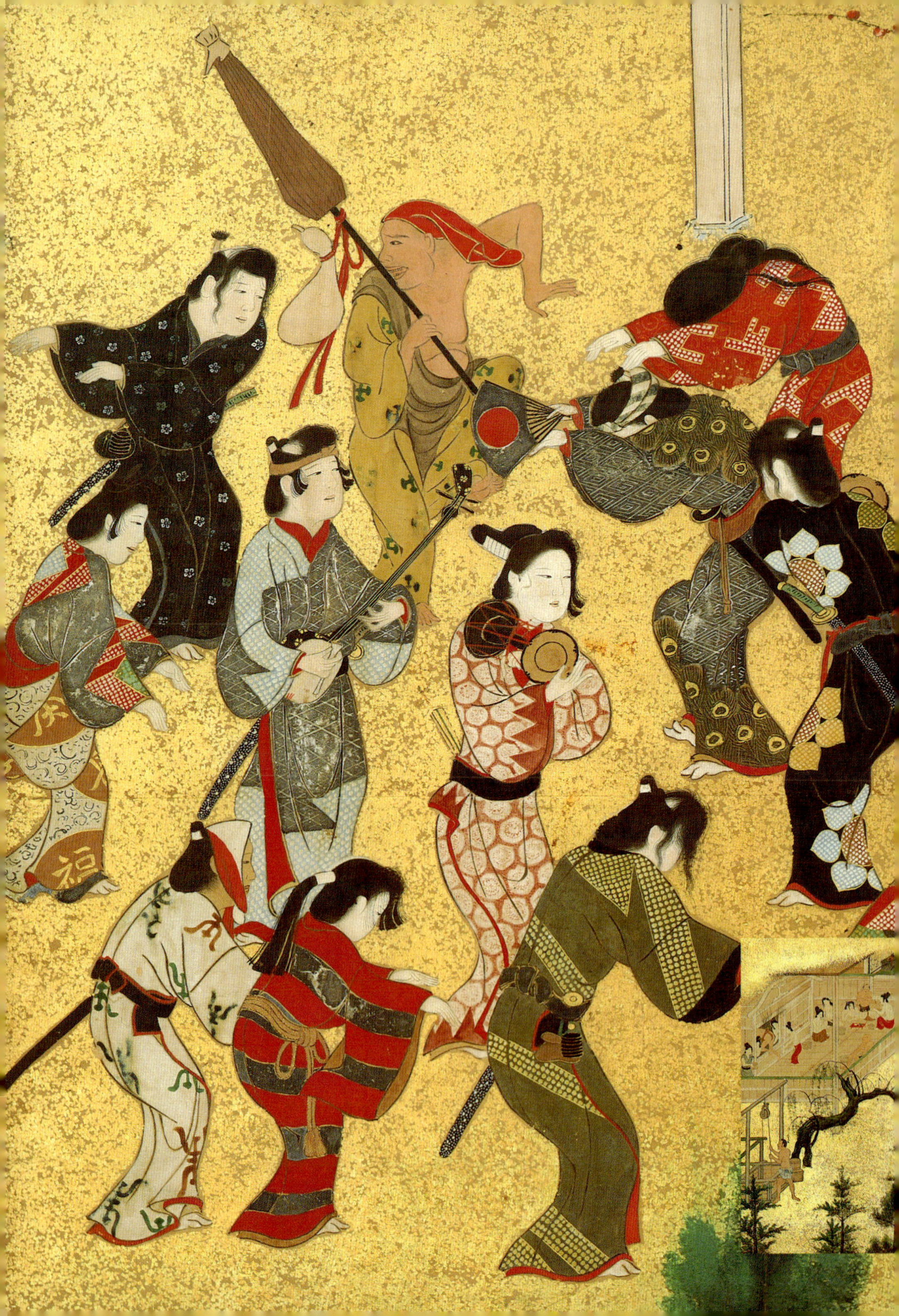

99 邸内遊楽図屏風　六曲一隻
東京・サントリー美術館
Scenes from the Gay Quarters.
Six-fold screen. Color on paper.
Early Edo period. 82.0×274.7cm
Suntory Museum of Art, Tokyo

100 白地幾何学鋸歯文様更紗陣羽織(山鹿素行所用)
長崎・松浦史料博物館
Jinbaori coat with design of geometrical and sawtooth pattern on a white ground. Worn by Yamaga Sokō.
Cotton: printed and mordant-dyed. 17c. Made in early Edo period. 99.0×58.3cm
Matsuura Historical Museum, Nagasaki.

101 更紗飛龍菊陣羽織 （前田慶寧所用） 東京・前田育徳会
Jinbaori coat with design of a plum. Worn by Maeda Yoshiyasu
Wool and cotton: painted, mordant-dyed and wax-resist. 17c. Made in
late Edo period. 107.0×42.0cm
Maeda Ikutokukai Foundation, Tokyo

ヨーロッパ産

ヨーロッパへもたらされたインド更紗は、その需要の拡大にともなって輸入超過に悩んでいた。模造更紗を作ることが試みられたのは当然で、1648年マルセイユにあるトランプ業者がその木版彫刻の技術を使って始めた。それがヨーロッパ各地に伝播し、銅版、シルクスクリーンと技術改良が進められて今日のヨーロッパプリントの源となった。

Made in Europe

An ever-growing demand for Indian *sarasa*-chintz caused a trade deficit in Europe. This encouraged Europeans to begin producing their own *sarasa*. In 1648, a card maker in Marseille started manufacturing *sarasa* utilizing the woodblock technology. Various improvements were made which led to the birth of existing European printing techniques.

102 赤地草花文様更紗茶具敷
Floor covering for the tea ceremony with design of flowers on a red ground.
Cotton: printed. 18-19c.

103 赤地草花文様更紗陣羽織
Jinbaori coat with design of flowers on a red ground.
Cotton: printed. 18-19c.

104 白地花鳥文様更紗
    Fragment with design of flowers and birds on a white ground.
    Cotton: printed. 18-19c.

105 藍地花果鳥虫文様更紗
    Floor covering with design of flowers, fruit, birds and insects on an indigo blue ground.
    Cotton: printed. 18-19c.

106 茶地草花文様更紗
    Fragment with design of flowers on a brown ground.
    Cotton: printed. 18-19c.

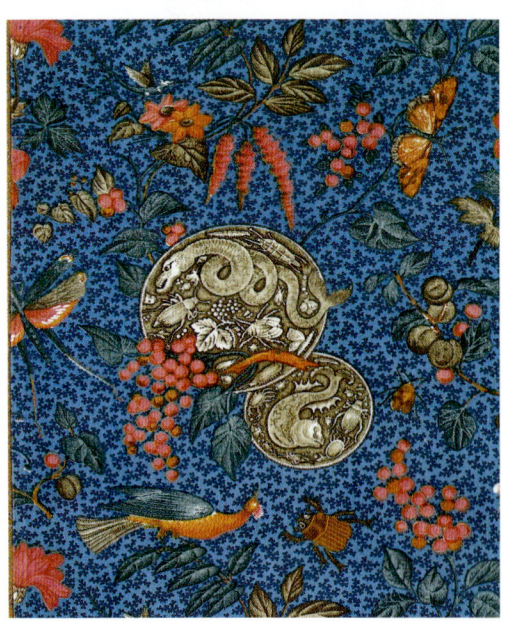

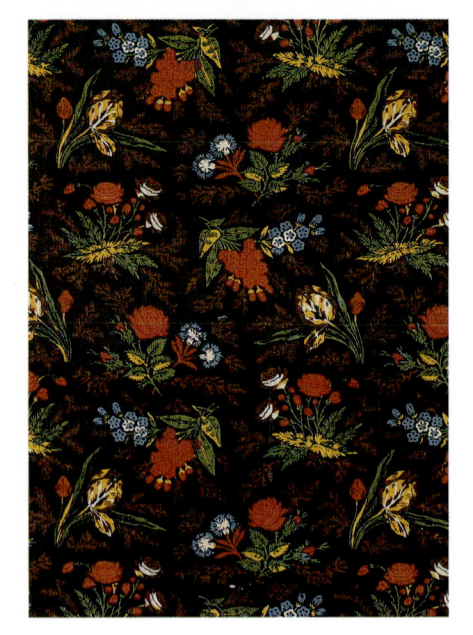

107　藍地草花風景文樣更紗
Fragment with design of flowers and landscape on an indigo blue ground.
Cotton: printed. 18-19c.

108　赤地草花楼閣文樣更紗
Fragment with design of flowers and buildings on a red ground.
Cotton: printed. 18-19c.

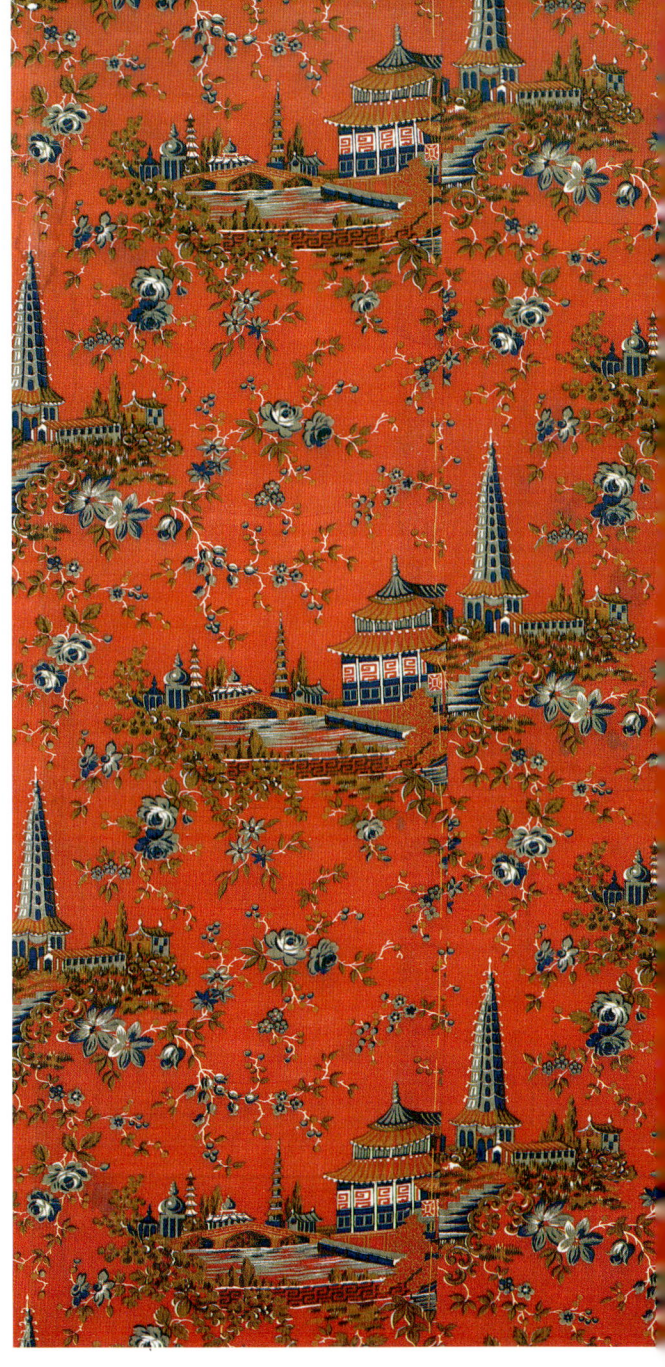

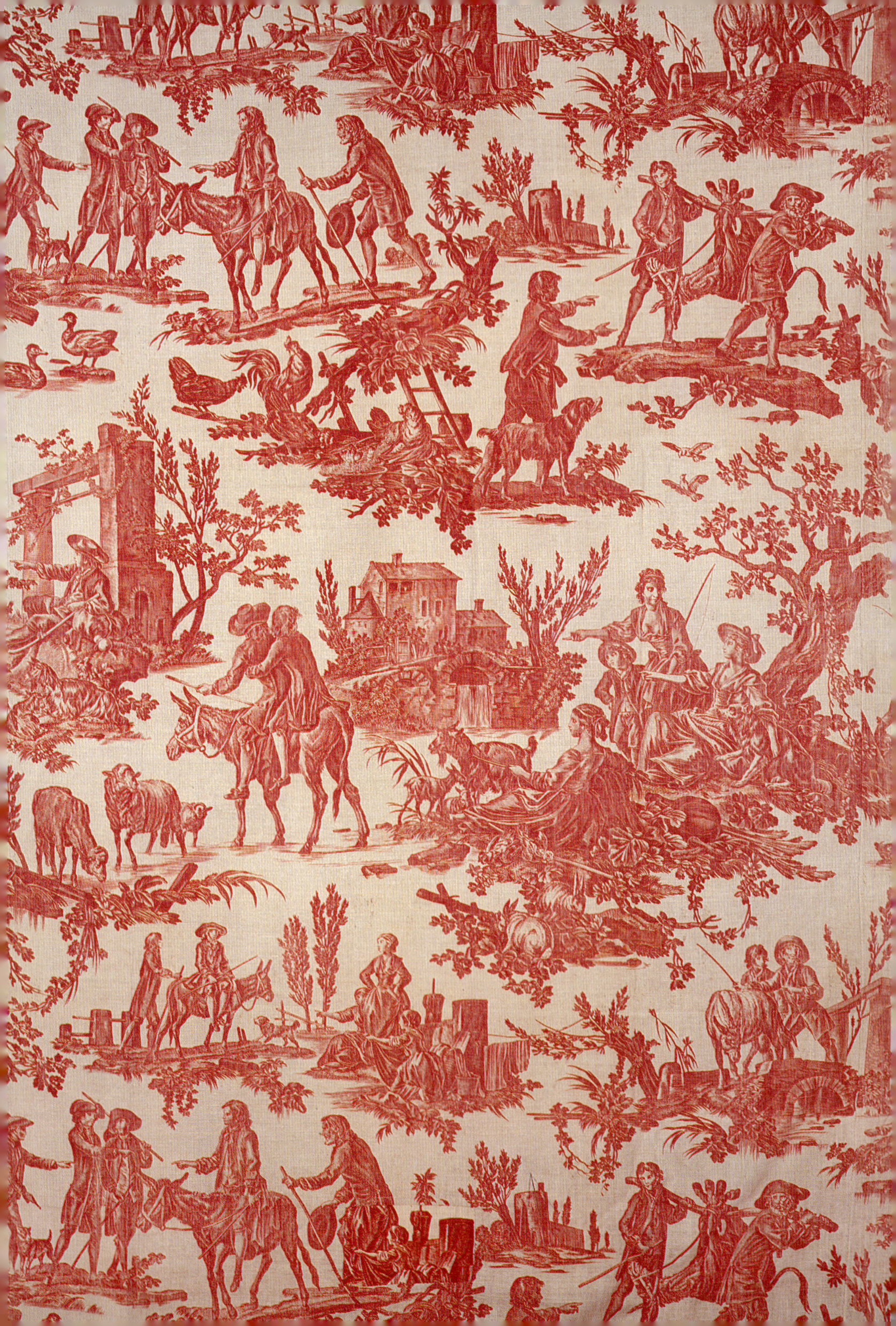

110 白地草花縞文様更紗下着
兵庫・神戸市立博物館
Underwear with design of vertical stripes of flowers on a white ground.
Cotton: Printed in Europe. 19c. Made in late Edo period. 151.5×59.0cm
Kōbe City Museum, Hyōgo.

109 白地草花人物鳥獣文様更紗
Fragment with design of flowers, figures, birds and animals on a white ground.
Cotton: printed. 18-19c.

和更紗

インドから輸入された更紗に刺激されて、日本の国内でも模造更紗が作られるようになった。京都、堺、長崎、鍋島などでそれぞれの地名を冠した名称で呼ばれている。ただ、茜の染料がないこと、その技術が不明であったことなどから、日本特産の型染の技法を応用、色彩は群青、弁柄など顔料を摺りこんだもので、水洗には弱いものであった。

Made in Japan

The influence of Indian *sarasa*-chintz led the Japanese to attempt to produce their own fabric. Since madder was not grown in Japan and Indian technology was unknown, they adapted an already known stencil-dyeing technique, but it lacked the colorfastness inherent in the Indian fabric.

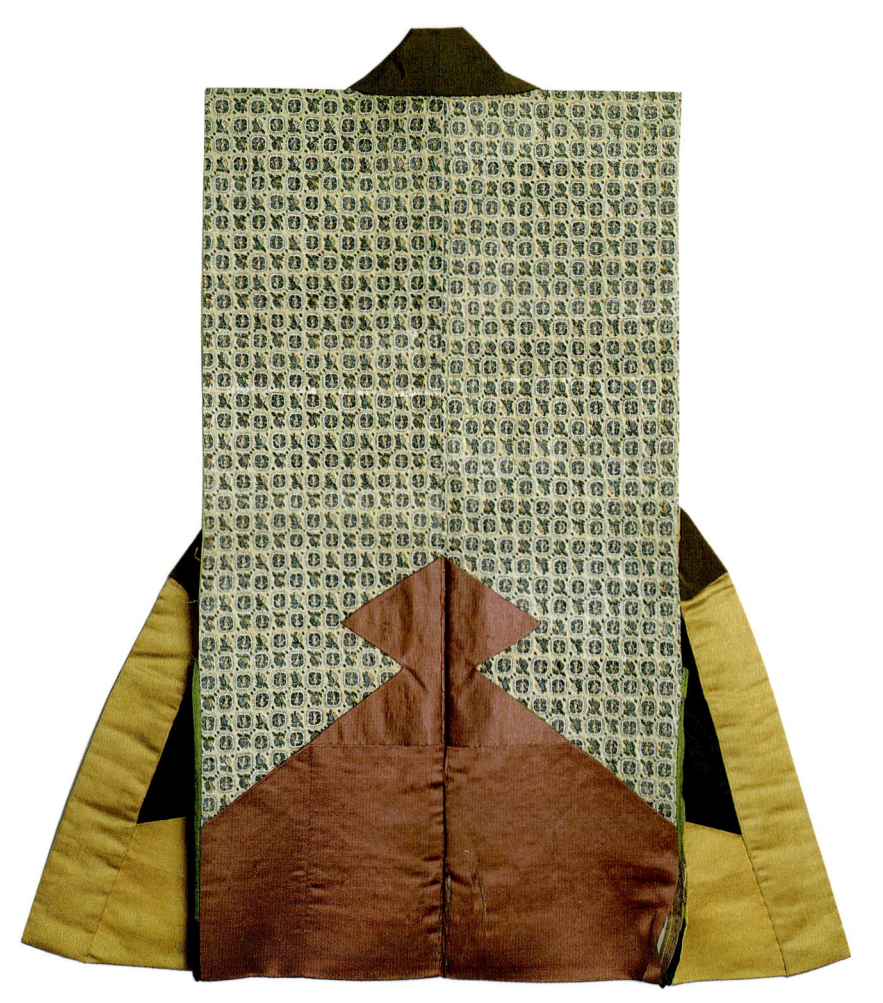

111 紙衣更紗に緞子松皮取り茶式衣
Vest for the tea ceremony. Paper and silk: stencilled by pigment. 18-19c.

京・堺更紗

主に京・堺で製造された和更紗で群青、黄土、弁柄などの顔料を型紙の上から摺り込む技法であった。

Kyō/Sakai *Sarasa*

These fabrics were made by rubbing pigments of ultramarine, yellow ocher and red oxide on the paper stencil-covered fabric.

112 白地菊手鞠文様更紗
Fragment with design of chrysanthemums and *temari* balls on a white ground.
Cotton: stencilled by pigment. 18-19c.

113 藍地唐花文様更紗
Fragment with design of Chinese style flowers on an indigo blue ground.
Cotton: stencilled by pigment. 18-19c.

長崎更紗

唐人紺屋で作られ、中国風の文様や西洋人物などが表わされる。染料の蘇芳を沈澱させ、顔料化したもの。赤茶色が特色。

Nagasaki *Sarasa*

This fabric was produced by a Chinese dyer and features Chinese designs and figures of Westerners. The reddish-brown color was created by precipitating sapanwood dye and turning it into a pigment.

114 赤地鳳凰唐草祇園山鉾文様更紗
兵庫・神戸市立博物館
Wrapper with design of phoenix, arabesque and festival float (Gion festival) on a red ground.
Cotton: stencilled by pigment and dyes.
Late Edo period. 91.5×93.0cm
Kōbe City Museum, Hyōgo.

115 白地紅毛人物花唐草文様更紗
Fragment with design of Dutchmen and arabesque on a white ground.
Cotton: stencilled by pigment and dyes.
Late Edo period.

鍋島更紗

鍋島では、藩の政策で更紗製作が保護された。色彩は長崎とほぼ同様であるが型紙だけでなく、一部には木版も併用した。

Nabeshima *Sarasa*

The feudal domain of Nabeshima encouraged the manufacture of *sarasa*. The coloration resembles that of the cloth produced in Nagasaki. Both stencil dyeing and woodblock prints were employed.

116 薄茶地大唐花文様更紗（鍋島更紗見本帖の内） 佐賀県立博物館
Fragment with design of Chinese style flowers on a light brown ground from the sample book of Nabeshima-*Sarasa*.
Cotton: stencilled by pigment. 18-19c.
Saga Prefectural Museum.

117 白地大唐花文様更紗（鍋島更紗見本帖の内） 佐賀県立博物館
Fragment with design of Chinese style flowers on a white ground from the sample book of Nabeshima-*Sarasa*.
Cotton: stencilled by pigment. 18-19c.
Saga Prefectural Museum.

ペルシャ産

回教のインドへの進出にともなって、染織においてもカシミアショール、更紗などの技術の交流が頻繁になり、古都イスパハンを中心にインドと同様のものが生産されるようになった。ただ文様的には生命樹を細かに配したものが多く、自ずから特徴が出ている。

Made in Persia

The spread of the Islamic culture to India stimulated weaving and dyeing technologies. In and around the ancient city of Ispahan, fabrics similar to Indian *sarasa*-chintz began to be produced. Persian *sarasa* features the elaborate tree-of-life motif.

118 白地草花文様更紗
Wall hanging with design of flowers on a white ground. Cotton: painted, mordant-dyed and wax-resist. 18-19c. 137.0×93.0cm

119 茜霜降地草花文様祈祷更紗
Wall hanging with design of flowers on a white ground. Cotton: printed, painted, mordant-dyed and wax-resist. 18-19c. 214.0×540.0cm

インドネシア産

インドネシアも更紗に刺激をうけた地で、かつては素朴に作られていた臈纈染が、その影響により緻密で華やかなものへと変わっていった。今やバティックすなわちジャワ更紗は世界中の臈纈の総称となっている。

Made in Indonesia; *Batik*

The indigenous wax-resist dye process of Indonesia gradually yielded rich, sophisticated fabrics through the influence of Indian *sarasa*-chintz. Today, *batik*, or Java *sarasa*, has become a generic term referring to all categories of wax-resist dyeing in the world.

120 赤地天使月桂冠文様更紗
Fragment with design of angels, laurel crowns and boats on a red ground.
Cotton: wax-resist (*batik* tulis) and painted. 20c.

121 藍地花鳥文様更紗
Fragment with design of flowers and birds on an indigo blue ground.
Cotton: wax-resist (*batik* tulis). 20c.

122 白地幾何学草花文様更紗
Fragment with design of geometrical pattern and flowers on a white ground.
Cotton: wax-resist (*batik* tulis). 20c.

85

インド更紗の染色法

Dyeing Technique for Indian *Sarasa*-chintz

木綿は、天然染料による鮮やかな赤や紫が染まりにくいという性質をもっている。インドでは、こうした木綿布に赤を主調とした美しい色彩を染めるため、古くから次のような極めて化学的な工程が行われていた。まず木綿にはよく染まる茶系のタンニン酸の染料で下染めし、明礬(Al)あるいは鉄漿(Fe)の媒染剤を付着しやすくしておく。これは、タンニン酸を染める時は必ず先に染料で染めてから、媒染剤で発色するという理論を応用したものである。そして木版あるいはカラムペンなどで、布の表面にそれらの媒染剤をしっかりと染着させるのである。茜は、はじめに媒染剤を付けたのち染めると発色するので、こうして媒染剤を染着した部分は美しい赤色が得られるというわけである。

Since quite early in their history, Indians developed a chemical process to dye cotton cloth a beautiful red and purple, although cotton by nature is hard to dye in these colors with natural dyes. First, the cloth is dyed with a tannic acid dye to facilitate the adhesion of mordants such as alum and iron acetate. Then, using a drawing pen called *kalam* (*qalam*) or a woodblock, the mordant is quickly applied fast onto the cloth. This is followed by dyeing it using madder dye. Only the portion of cloth where the mordant is applied, is dyed a beautiful madder red color.

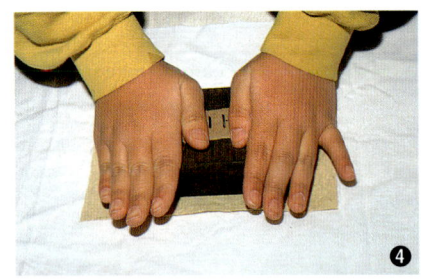

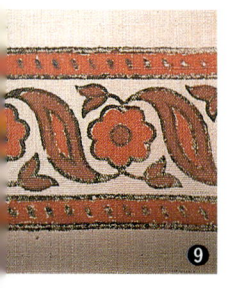

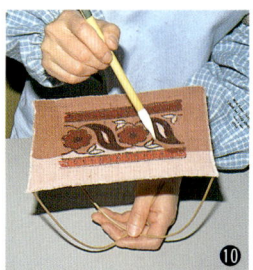

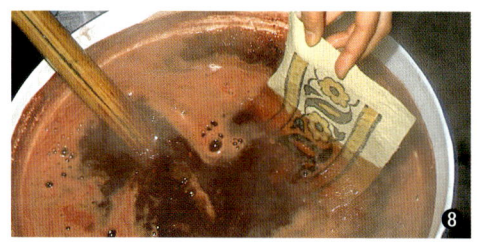

① 乾燥したミロバランの果実。
② ①を煮沸して抽出液をとる。
③ ②の抽出液に木綿布を浸してうすく染める（タンニン酸下染）。
④ ③の布を乾燥させた後、文様の輪郭を表した木版に、鉄漿を付けて捺す（鉄媒染）。
⑤ 鉄漿による輪郭線。この線は黒く仕上がる。
⑥ 輪郭の枠内で、茜色にしたい部分に明礬を塗る（明礬媒染）。
⑦ さらに、紫色にしたい部分には鉄漿と明礬の混合液を塗る（鉄・明礬媒染）。
⑧ 布全体を、80℃に保った六葉茜の染液に浸して染める。
⑨ 水洗し、発色させたところ。
⑩ 藍色にしたい部分を残して、全体に臈を塗る（臈防染）。
⑪ 藍の染液に浸して染める。
⑫ 酸化させて完成。

① Dried myrobalan fruit.
② They are boiled in water to produce an extract.
③ The cotton cloth is immersed in the extract, and dyed a pale color.
④ After the cloth is dried, the outline of the pattern is printed, using a woodblock to which iron acetate has been applied.
⑤ The outline is dyed black.
⑥ Alum is applied on the portion to be dyed madder.
⑦ A mixture of alum and iron acetate is applied on the portion to be dyed purple.
⑧ The entire cloth is immersed in a liquid dye of Indian madder which is kept at 80°C.
⑨ Beautiful colors appear after the cloth is rinsed in water.
⑩ The portion which is to be dyed indigo is reserved, and wax is applied to the remainder.
⑪ The entire cloth is immersed in an indigo dye bath.
⑫ Finally, the beautifully dyed fabric is oxidized and dried.

更紗について

吉岡幸雄

更紗の発生と伝播

　「さらさ」という、言葉の響きがいかにも異国情緒をかきたてる染織品は、インドにおいて古くから生産されていた茜色の華麗な木綿布のことで、それが世界の各地へ運ばれると多大な人気を博し、広く愛用されてきた。

　日本へは十六〜十七世紀にもたらされたとされ、それ以後、長い間にわたって日本人の眼を魅了しつづけている。

　その染色技術の源がインドである更紗をこの「日本の染織」のシリーズにとりあげるのは、日本人の生活のなかに多くとり入れられて技術的にも大きな刺激と影響を与えてきたからに他ならない。ここではインドで生産された更紗の特殊な技術とそれがどのように世界各地に受容されたのかを日本を中心として記すものである。

　そもそもインド更紗とはどのような染織品をさすのか。インドは周知のように紀元前2500年より、インダス川流域のパンジャブ地方を中心として、世界四大文明の一つインダス文明が形成されており、早くから開けた地であったが、染織の歴史において注目されるのは木綿の栽培の技術をいち早く完成させていたことである。

　木綿は丈夫でいくたびの洗濯にも耐え柔らかく保温性があるというように、人間の衣料にとって極めて優秀な繊維であるが、その一方で色を付けるための植物染料は藍と茶、くすんだ黄色以外は染着させることが困難であるため、多彩な色と文様を表わすことが出来なかったのである。

　しかし、インドでは遅くとも紀元前後にはこの木綿布に赤、紫などの華やかな染色を行なうことが考え出されていた。その詳細は86・87頁の工程で記したのでそれを参照されたいが、極めて化学的な工夫がなされていることに驚かされる。

　こうして彩色された木綿布は、その華やかな色彩でもって注目をあび、長きにわたって輸出品として諸地域へ運ばれていった。だがそれが本格的な貿易品として広く世界に流布したのは、十五世紀以降の航海術の発達によるヨーロッパ人の東洋への進出によってであった。香辛料をはじめとする神秘的な東洋の産物を求めてのインド航路の発見は、更紗の世界への流通にも大いに貢献したのであった。

　木綿は現在ではどこの国々でも使われている一般的な衣料であるが、十四、五世紀までのヨーロッパは十字軍の遠征などにより、わずかにその存在を知っただけである。また、インドより東の中国、日本なども、同じ頃にはようやくその栽培が始まったばかりで、どちらかといえばなじみの薄い繊維であ

った。

　だが、保温性にとみ、水分の吸収力も優れた木綿に赤色を中心として華やかに彩色された更紗がもたらされると、大きな反響を呼びおこし多大な人気を博した。こうして東西での更紗及び木綿の受容はそれぞれの地の服飾に、いささか大げさに表現すれば革命的な影響を与えたといえよう。
　では、日本へはいつの頃よりインド更紗がもたらされたのであろうか。
　確かな文献ではイギリス東インド会社の船長ジョン・セーリスがその航海日記(1613年)に記した、平戸の領主にインド更紗四端を贈った記録が初見とされてきたが、これ以前にも日本にもたらされたと想定できる資料がある。それは、いわゆる南蛮貿易が開始される以前の琉球列島を中心とする南島との通交貿易に関するもので、その資料の中に「上水花布」「西洋紅布」「緋色木綿」などの記載があり、このほかポルトガルの派遣大使トメ・ピレスが1511年から1513年にかけてインド及びマラッカに旅した時の記録『東方諸国記』の中で、レケオ(琉球人のこと、レキオに同じ)に触れて、「毎年マラカには一隻ないし二、三隻のジュンコ(船)がやってきて、ベンガラ産の衣服を大量に持ち帰る。(中略)レキオ人は七、八日でジャンポン(日本の本土の意)に赴き、上記の商品を携えて行く。……」と記している。かつて沖縄にはその地理的な条件から、中国福建省、タイ、マラッカなどのインドシナ半島、インドネシア、フィリピンを季節風にのって回航する船があり、それが先の記録にあるように中国、東南アジア諸地域と貿易を行なっていたわけである。
　日本へ更紗が貿易品として本格的に輸入されるようになったのは、江戸時代の初め頃と考えられる。先の『セーリス日本航海記』に次いで1614年に平戸に来航した英国商館員の書簡類にPintado(さらさの意味)の記述があり、平戸にあるオランダ商館の帳簿類、『唐蛮貨物帳』などに「さらさ二四七五端」など多くの記載が見られる。
　こうした十七世紀初めの文献の記事を裏付けるように、年代が明らかな更紗の現存する資料をいくつか見ることができる。
　加賀百万石前田家には、数多い名物裂が伝来し、そのなかにいくつかのインド更紗がある。そのうちの一つが「白地獅子草花蛇文様金更紗」(図版74)で、白地にカラムペンによって極めて精緻に、かつのびやかな線が描かれ、立体感を出すように色彩の濃淡も繊細なグラデーションで表され、線描の上には濃密な金が置かれている、世界にもあまり類を見ない名品である。
　この「金華布」と通称されるものは、記録によると三代前田利常が寛永十四年(1637)に眼ききの商人にわざわざ長崎に出向かせて購入したとされている。さらに現在は平戸松浦史料博物館に収蔵される白地に鋸歯文が描かれたインド更紗の陣羽織(図版100)があり、江戸時代の初めの古学派の儒学者であり兵学者であった山鹿素行(1622〜85)が所用していたと伝えられている。また、長い歴史を誇る京都祇園祭は十六世紀から十七世紀にかけての近世の

初頭、富める町衆たちが競って鉾や山の装飾に華やかな輸入裂を求めたようで、ベルギー製のタピスリー、ペルシャの絨緞などに混じってインド更紗もいくつか見られる。なかでも南観音山に伝えられる「茜地草花文様更紗敷物」(図版75)は、かつて見送りに用いられていたもので、裏地に「貞享元年(1684)甲子六月吉日南観音山袋屋庄兵衛内」の墨書があり、その年に寄進されたとわかる貴重な資料である。

　江戸期の風俗画にもいくつか更紗が描かれているものがあり、その代表的なものを拾ってみると、サントリー美術館収蔵の寛永年間(1624～44)に描かれたとされる「邸内遊楽図」屏風(図版99)には、更紗を着た人物が描かれている。またＭＯＡ美術館には慶安年間(1648～52)の「誰が袖図」屏風(図版98)があり、このほか尾張徳川家には仕覆に用いられた残りと見られる更紗裂(図版29・30)が伝えられ、彦根井伊家に伝えられた、通称彦根更紗(現在、東京国立博物館保管　図版37～43ほか)には四百五十種にも及ぶ江戸時代に輸入された更紗の裂が集められている。さらに細川家には更紗の茶杓の袋(図版84～89)なども見られ、かなりの大名、旧家などで更紗が用いられていたことがわかる。

更紗の文様と日本の染色への影響

　インドにおいて染められた更紗は布地の種類と技法によって二つに大別できる。一つは、細く繊維の長い良質の木綿糸を強く打ち込んだ目のつまった布に、カラムペンを用いて手描きで細密な文様を表し、茜染を主とした更紗染色を行い、さらに青と緑系の色彩を出すために臈伏せして藍で浸染した手の込んだ上手のもので、もう一つはやや太い甘撚りの木綿糸をやや粗く織った厚手の木綿布に、主に木版を用いて型押しして染色したいわゆる鬼更紗系のものである。後者は日本では敷物や風呂敷などに多く用いられている。

　文様については、インドはかなり古くより染織品の輸出国であり、輸出先の各地域の好みや用途に応じたもの、たとえばシャム(タイ国)の寺院用には仏手、ヨーロッパ向けには人物文様も変えるなどして制作している。日本においても扇面、縞、小花文などが現存しており、日本向けのものを特に生産していたと考えられる。一枚の更紗の両端のＷの形、つまり鋸歯文はインドネシア向けが中心と考えられたが、江戸期の絵画資料や現存するものを見てみると、一枚の布の上下にはほとんどきまってこの文様を配し、その中央部に様々な文様を配置していたように考えられる。

　そうした一方で、京都祇園祭南観音山に伝来する「茜地鶴松山水文様更紗」の胴掛け(図版44)と同じような文様が、かつてはオランダ本国にも伝来し、現在、アメリカ、ニューヨーク市のクーパー・ヒューウィット博物館及びカナダのトロント市ロイヤル・オンタリオ博物館にも収蔵されている。つまり、オランダ、イギリスなどの東インド会社(Ｖ・Ｏ・Ｃ／Ｅ・Ｉ・Ｃ)における

更紗の貿易では日本向けの文様に限らず異国情緒豊かなものも輸入され、大いに日本人のあこがれを誘っていたと思われる。

やや時代が下るが、安永七年(1778)に『佐羅紗便覧』、同十年(1781)に『増補華布便覧』、天明五年(1785)には『更紗図譜』が相次いで発行された。これらはいずれも古渡更紗の裂の断片の文様を木版で表し、生﨟脂、藍臈、雌黄、紫、墨、金など彩色を文字で示して、巻末にその技法が記されている。だがその技法もインド本来の更紗の文様と色彩を表しながら、それを友禅の技法で表現しているところが興味深い。こうした書物から見てもわかるように、元禄時代(1688～1704)に発生した友禅染の白揚げの細い曲線の表現方法、赤色を中心とする色彩、さらには今日伝来する友禅の名品に見られる文様の細部など、友禅染と更紗染色には互いの共通項が多く見られることに注目される。さらに同じ頃発生した沖縄の紅型と見まちがえるような文様もあって(図版40参照)、更紗が日本の染色に与えた影響はかなり大きかったといえよう。

そして、江戸時代中期以後、インド更紗の輸入の増大につれて、ヨーロッパやジャワなどと同様にその模造品が日本でも生産されるようになった。

その輸入のありさまをつぶさに見ていた長崎出島の唐人紺屋、さらに佐賀鍋島藩、堺、京都などで十七世紀の終わり頃には、早くも生産されていたと考えられる。正保二年(1645)刊の『毛吹草』には「紗羅染」が山城(京都)の名産と記され、堺では元禄年間にさらさ染屋があった、という記録が遺っている。ただ、総称して「和更紗」と呼ばれるこれらはいずれも、技法的にはインドと同じ六葉茜などの染料がないところから、顔料あるいは蘇芳などの染料を顔料化したものを用い、日本の特産である染型紙を使って摺り込む技法(鍋島では木版も併用されていた)が採られていて、洗濯などにあまり強度のあるものではなかった。用途は富裕な人々が用いる蒲団地や風呂敷などが多かったようである。

こうして見るとインドより順次東進してきた木綿の栽培によって、江戸時代の人々が日常の衣生活において、かなり豊かになって、藍染の型染、紺絣のような技法によってその彩りを楽しんだ一方、武家や富める町人達はインドで彩色された茜色の更紗を輸入して茶道具の仕覆や衣裳として異国の情緒を味わっていたのである。それがまた江戸時代の友禅や和更紗にも影響を与え、今日もなお日本人にとって更紗に対する思いの深さが継続しているといえようか。

(よしおかさちお　染織研究家)

Sarasa, printed and painted textiles

YOSHIOKA Sachio

The Birth and Propagation of *Sarasa*-chintz

Sarasa, a term which sounds extremely exotic to Japanese ears, refers to madder-colored cotton fabrics which were produced in India from ancient times. Transported to various regions of the world, these fabrics soon became popular and enjoyed wide usage. Supposedly, *sarasa*-chintz was brought to Japan in the 16th or 17th century, and ever since, it has appealed aestheticly to the Japanese.

Sarasa-chintz, a dyeing technique which was first developed in India, is included in this series on "Japanese Textiles" because of its great influence and stimulus to the dyeing technologies in Japan making it an inseparable part of Japanese textile traditions. This volume records the unique technique of *sarasa*-chintz which India produced, a technique that has been widely accepted throughout the world, and makes special mention of the fabric's history in Japan.

The Indus civilization, one of the four great civilizations of mankind, flourished in the Punjab district of the Indus River basin from the earliest times in the history of man. The establishment of the cultivation of cotton in India is a remarkable event in the world's history of textiles.

Strong, washable and warm, cotton is one of the world's most useful fibers. However, in ancient times, there was one drawback: vegetable pigments only yielded the colors of indigo, brown or dull yellow, making it impossible to create interesting patterns in a variety of colors.

By the first century, the technology to dye cotton cloth in red, purple and other beautiful colors had evolved in India. It is astonishing to realize that, at this time in history, a chemical process already had been developed and was widely employed. (For more information, please refer to the dyeing process described on pages 86-87)

Dyed in attractive colors, cotton fabrics gained such popularity that they soon became an important trade item, and for hundreds of years, were transported to various parts of the world. This transport was made possible by the remarkable development of navigation in and after the 15th century, enabling the Europeans to reach the Orient. The discovery of a sea route to India by Europeans seeking to obtain spices and other exotic products of the Orient greatly contributed to the spread of *sarasa*-chintz thoughout the world.

Although today cotton is commonly used by everyone, before the 14th or 15th century Europeans only knew of its existence through the Crusaders. In China and Japan, cotton cultivation was begun in the 14th or 15th century, and it was not a popular fiber.

Sarasa-chintz dyed in red and other beautiful colors with warmth-retention and water-absorbing properties, was highly attractive and considered wondrous. Cotton and *sarasa*-chintz had a "revolutionary" influence on clothing both in the Occident and the Orient.

A concise despription of Indian *sarasa*-chintz first appears in the "Voyage of Captain John Saris to Japan" (1613). According to this logbook of Saris', a captain of the British East India Company, Indian *sarasa*-chintz was given as a gift to the feudal lord of Hirado. There remain other old documents which imply that *sarasa*-chintz had been brought to Japan before that time. Words such as "Western red fabric" and "crimson cotton" appear in a document describing Japan's trade with its southern islands, particularly Ryūkyū, and just before its comencement of official trade with foreign countries (*namban bōeki*). Furthermore, "Suma Oriental que trata do Maar Roxo ate os Chins," a record of a journey in India and Malacca by the Portuguese ambassador Tomé Pires from 1511 to 1513, contains the description: "Ryūkyūans visiting Malacca took Bengali clothes to Japan for sale. Long ago, ships that were engaged in trade between China and Southeast Asian countries sailed with the seasonal winds from the Fujien coast of China, to Thailand, Malacca, the Indochina peninsula, Indonesia and the Philippines as well as Okinawa.

It is believed that *sarasa*-chintz began to be imported into Japan in the early Edo period. After the above-mentioned record of Captain Saris' voyage, the term "Pintado" (meaning *sarasa*-chintz) appeared in a letter written by an employee of an English trading house who visited Hirado in 1614, and again in a number of descriptions of *sarasa*-chintz in the ledgers of a Dutch trading company which had an office in Hirado. These early 17th century descriptions of *sarasa*-chintz are confirmed by the existence of fabrics whose production dates are known.

The head of the Maeda family, the formal feudal lord of Kaga province (located in the southern part of present-day Ishikawa Prefecture), has several pieces of *sarasa*-chintz in a collection of *meibutsu-gire* (celebrated fabrics) which has been handed in that family. Among the *sarasa*-chintz is a "fragment with the design of lions, snakes and flowers on a white ground" (Plate 74). The patterns are painted freely yet meticulously with a *kalam* (*qalam*) or drawing pen on a white ground. In addition, colors are graduated subtly to add depth to the overall design. The motif is perfected by the addition of thick gold drawn on the lines. The rich and luxurious piece of *sarasa*-chintz is the only of its kind.

This particular piece, commonly referred to as "Kinka-fu," is said to have been purchased by Maeda Toshitsune, the third head of the Maeda family, who dispatched a connoisseur merchant to Nagasaki to buy the finest piece of cloth available in the 14th year of Kan'ei (1637). Another example is the "*Jimbaori* coat with the geometric design and sawtooth pattern on a white ground," which is now in the collection of the Matsuura Historical Museum in Hirado. This garment is said to have been worn by Yamaga Sokō (1622-1685), a renowned Confucian and tactician in the early Edo period. From the 16th and

17th centuries, wealthy merchants in Kyoto competed with each other to purchase rare imported fabrics to decorate the floats of the traditional Gion Festival. The decorative coverings include Belgian tapestries, Persian rugs, and Indian *sarasa*-chintz. On piece in particular is important because the year of donation and the donor are known from an ink inscription on its reverse side. It is the "hanging with floral design on madder red ground," which was used to decorate the Minami-kannonyama Float.

Sarasa was also depicted in genre paintings of the Edo period. Believed to have been completed during the Kan'ei era (1624-1644), the "Scenes from the Gay Quarters" (Plate 99), which is preserved in the Suntory Museum of Art, show a few figures in the crowd wearing *sarasa* kimono. Preserved in the MOA Museum of Art is the folding screen entitled, "*Tagasode* Screen" (Plate 98). It depicts a *sarasa* kimono among a other kinds of kimono. Furthermore, the Tokugawa family of Owari preserves fragments of *sarasa* which are said to be the remainders of the fabric covers for powdered green tea containers. The "Hikone *Sarasa*," long treasured by the Ii family of Hikone and now preserved in the Tokyo National Museum, contains about 450 different kinds of *sarasa* fabrics which were imported into Japan during the Edo period. Preserved by the Hosokawa family are *sarasa* cases for tea scoops used in the tea ceremony (Plates 84-89). This is an indication of the popularity of *sarasa* among *daimyō* and high ranking families of various provinces.

The Designs of *Sarasa*-chintz and their Influence on Japanese Textiles

Sarasa-chintz produced in India can be classified into two categories depending on the type of fabric used and the dyeing technique. One is an elaborate cloth of densely woven fine cotton fabric using thin, long cotton fibers on which minute patterns are painted free-hand with a *kalam* (*qalam*) drawing pen and dyed in madder red and other typical *sarasa* colors, and complemented by the addition of greenish and bluish tints using wax-resist indigo dye. The other type, generally called *oni-zarasa*, is thick and coarsely woven cloth using loosely twisted cotton yarn on which patterns are made with a woodblock print. *Sarasa*-chintz of the latter category is widely used as floor coverings or square-shaped cloth wrappers.

Concerning motifs, Indians, who were exporting textiles since ancient times, drew patterns according to the tastes of their customers and their subsequent use: e.g. geometric figures of Buddha were made for temples in Siam (Thailand) and figures of Westerners for European countries. In Japan, *sarasa*-chintz with fans, stripes and floral motifs have been preserved to date. It is presumed that Indians produced *sarasa*-chintz with patterns specially designed for Japan. *Sarasa*-chintz bordered with a sawteeth pattern along two sides was produced especially for Indonesia. However, judging from the Edo period paintings and *sarasa*-chintz preserved to date, almost all *sarasa*-chintz fabrics seem to have a sawteeth pattern, the space between the sawteeth being filled with a variety of typical *sarasa* patterns.

Sarasa-chintz fabrics similar in pattern to the "hanging with design of cranes, pine trees and landscape" used for the Minami-kannonyama Float in the Gion Festival were once taken to Holland, and are now in the collections of the Cooper Hewitt Museum in New York and the Royal Ontario Museum in Toronto. As a result of trade conducted by the British East Indian Company and its Dutch counterpart (Vereenighde Oost Indische Compagnie), not only *sarasa*-chintz designed for Japanese, but those produced for Westerners were brought to Japan, influencing Japanese taste for European design.

Following the publication of "Sarasa Benran" in the 7th year of An'ei (1778), various *sarasa*-chintz manuals for dyers of *wa-zarasa* and Yūzen were published in quick succession. In all these manuals, the patterns of old *sarasa*-chintz fabrics imported to Japan were reproduced by woodblock print and the colors for cochineal, indigo, gamboge, purple, ink-black, gold and so forth were written in Chinese characters. At the end of each manual, the technique of *sarasa*-chintz is explained. It is intriguing that the technique described in those manuals was that of Yūzen dyeing while the patterns and colors were that of authentic Indian *sarasa*-chintz. Looking at these old documents, it is astonishing that there are many elements common to *sarasa*-chintz and Yūzen dyeing, a technique which was developed in the Genroku era (1688-1704). Yūzen is a technique that reserved fine lines in white, used a red-based coloration, and incorporated detailed patterns. Furthermore, some patterns of *bingata* dyeing in Okinawa were developed about the same time and resemble *sarasa*-chintz patterns. All these indicate the great influence that *sarasa*-chintz had on Japanese dyeing techniques.

In and after the mid-Edo period, with the ever-increasing imports of Indian *sarasa*-chintz, imitation products began to appear in Japan, as they did in Europe and Java. European dyers residing in Dejima (a residential quarters for Westerners) in Nagasaki and Japanese dyers in Nabeshima, Sakai and Kyoto, began to produce imitation *sarasa*-chintz by the end of the 17th century. "Kefukigusa," a book published in the 2nd year of Seiho (1645) contains the record that "shamurozome," which means *sarasa*-chintz, was an indigenous product of Yamashiro (present-day Kyoto Prefecture) and also that some dyers were engaged in the prouduction of *sarasa* in Sakai in the Genroku era. The dyeing technique employed for these products, generally referred to as *wa-zarasa*, differs from the original Indian technique. Since Indian madder was not available in Japan, the Japanese had to use pigments or dye-based pigments, such as sappanwood. In addition, the technique of stencil dyeing was employed in Japan. (In Nabeshima, woodbloock printing was also employed.) Due to these technical constraints, *sarasa* produced in Japan was not as water-resistant as the Indian variety, and thereby, primarily used as wrapping cloths and bed covers for the wealthy. With the gradual propagation of cotton cultivation from India to East Asia, commoners in the Edo period wore clothing in their everyday lives made with indigo stencil dyes and ikat while the samurai class and the rich merchants had access to Indian-made madder-colored *sarasa*-chintz for their clothing as well as for items such as tea container covers. This wide usage invariably influenced Yūzen dyeing and *wa-zarasa*. Even today, the Japanese love of *sarasa* is as strong as ever.

◆制作協力

逸翁美術館／永青文庫／ＭＯＡ美術館／鐘紡繊維美術館／京都国立博物館／鯉山保存会／神戸市立博物館／今昔・西村／佐賀県立博物館／三彩工芸／サントリー美術館／たばこと塩の博物館／東京国立博物館／徳川美術館／徳川黎明会／彦根城博物館／文化学園服飾博物館／前田育徳会／松浦資料博物館／南観音山保存会／恋壺洞／岩佐静子／岡田一郎／カマール・ヴィジャヴァルギヤ／畑中基良／柳孝／藪本公三

◆Cooperation

Bunka Gakuen Costume Museum, Tokyo / Eisei Bunko Museum, Tokyo / Hikone Castle Museum, Shiga / Itsuō Art Museum, Osaka / Kanebō Museum of Textiles, Osaka / Kōbe City Museum, Hyōgo / Koiyama Festival Preservation Society, Kyoto / Konjaku-Nishimura, Kyoto / Kyoto National Museum / Maeda Ikutokukai Foundation, Tokyo / Matuura Historical Museum, Nagasaki / Minami-kannonyama Festival Preservation Society, Kyoto / MOA Museum of Art, Shizuoka / Renkodō, Kyoto / Saga Prefectural Museum / Sansai Kōgei, Osaka / Suntory Museum of Art, Tokyo / Tobacco & Salt Museum, Tokyo / Tokugawa Art Museum, Aichi /Tokugawa Reimeikai, Tokyo / Tokyo National Museum / HATANAKA Motoyoshi / IWASA Shizuko / Kamal VIJAYVARGIYA, India / OKADA Ichirō / YABUMOTO Kōzō / YANAGI Takashi

・本書は、「京都書院美術双書　日本の染織20」-『更紗』（1993年7月発行）を新装本として再び刊行するものです。

・This publication is a newly bound edition of Kyoto Shoin's Art Library of Japanese Textiles Vol. 20: *Sarasa*, printed and painted textiles (first published in July 1993).

更紗

定価	［本体価格1,900円＋税］
発行	2014年5月1日
本文	吉岡幸雄
翻訳	下山あい ジュディス・A・クランシー
編集	紫紅社
発行者	勝丸裕哉
印刷	ニューカラー写真印刷株式会社
製本	藤原製本
発行所	紫紅社 〒605-0089 京都市東山区古門前通大和大路東入ル元町367 Tel.075-541-0206　Fax.075-541-0209

http://www.artbooks-shikosha.com/
©Shikosha, 2014　Printed in Japan.　ISBN978-4-87940-612-5

Sarasa, printed and painted textiles

Date of Publication	May 1, 2014
Author	YOSHIOKA Sachio
Translators	SHIMOYAMA Ai Judith A. CLANCY
Editor	Shikosha Co., Ltd.
Printer	New Color Photographic Printing Co., Ltd.
Book Binder	Fujiwara Bindery Co., Ltd.
Publisher	KATSUMARU Yuya Shikosha Co., Ltd. Motomachi 367, Yamato-oji, Higashi-iru Furumonzen, Higashiyama-ku, Kyoto, Japan 605-0089 Tel.075-541-0206 Fax.075-541-0209